# Progress in IS

More information about this series at http://www.springer.com/series/10440

Philipp Klöcker

# Resistance Behavior to National eHealth Implementation Programs

 Springer

Philipp Klöcker
Faculty of Business and Economics
University of Augsburg
Augsburg
Germany

ISSN 2196-8705                    ISSN 2196-8713    (electronic)
Progress in IS
ISBN 978-3-319-17827-1           ISBN 978-3-319-17828-8    (eBook)
DOI 10.1007/978-3-319-17828-8

Library of Congress Control Number: 2015937017

Springer Cham Heidelberg New York Dordrecht London

Printed on acid-free paper

Springer International Publishing AG Switzerland is part of Springer Science+Business Media
(www.springer.com)

# Acknowledgments

This thesis is the result of my work as a doctoral candidate at the University of Augsburg, School of Business and Economics, Chair of Information Systems and Management, Prof. Dr. Daniel Veit. I hereby want to thank all those who have generously supported me during this journey.

First of all, my deep gratitude goes to Prof. Dr. Daniel Veit for his constructive feedback and professional support throughout my time at his chair.

Secondly, I thank Dr. Rainer Bernnat for his hands-on, motivating, and honest counsel over the last years. Without his support this project would not have been possible.

I also want to express my heartfelt gratitude to Prof. Saonee Sarker and Prof. Suprateek Sarker for the academically insightful and personally enriching experience at the University of Virginia.

I thank my colleagues at the chair for challenging my ideas and sharing their expertise as well as their friendship. Special thanks go to Dr. Philipp Wunderlich, Dr. Jan Huntgeburth, Dr. Manuel Trenz, Dennis Steininger, Sabrina Hauff, Amelie Sach, An Bui, and Seda Alver.

Last but not least, thank you so much to my dear and loving family, my parents Ingo and Lucia, and my brother David. Thank you for believing in me. I know I can always count on you when it matters most!

Augsburg/Berlin                                                    Philipp Klöcker
2014

# Contents

# Abbreviations

| | |
|---|---|
| AVE | Average variance extracted |
| BfDI | Bundesbeauftragte für den Datenschutz und die Informationsfreiheit (Federal Commissioner for Data Protection and Freedom of Information) |
| BMG | Bundesministerium für Gesundheit (Federal Ministry of Health) |
| BSI | Bundesamt für Sicherheit in der Informationstechnik (Federal Office for Information Security) |
| CR | Composite reliability |
| DSL | Digital subscriber line |
| 'eGK' | elektronische Gesundheitskarte (Electronic health card) |
| 'eGK' technology | Refers to the whole of the associated technology including the front end installed at the medical practices as well as the backbone |
| EHR | Electronic health record |
| EPR | Electronic patient record |
| 'gematik' | Gesellschaft für Telematikanwendungen der Gesundheitskarte mbh (Society for Telematics Applications) |
| GDP | Gross domestic product |
| HBA | Heilberufsausweis (Health professional card) |
| HIE | Health information exchange |
| IS | Information system |
| KVK | Krankenversichertenkarte (Health insurance card) |
| mHealth | Mobile health |
| NCRS | NHS care record service |
| NHS | National health service |
| QES | Qualifizierte elektronische Signatur (Qualified electronic signature) |

| SEM | Structural equation model |
| UFS | Update flag service |
| UMTS | Universal mobile telecommunications service |
| VPN | Virtual private network |
| VSDM | Versichertenstammdatenmanagement (Patient master data) |

# List of Figures

# List of Tables

# Preamble

This doctoral thesis discusses the introduction of the electronic health card ('eGK') technology in Germany. I acknowledge that over the last years there has been some debate about the technology itself and the manner of its introduction.

This thesis does not aim at making practical recommendations to any parties involved in the rollout process on how to improve the technology or the implementation process. While my work reflects insights obtained from qualitative and quantitative data both gathered from various stakeholders involved in the rollout process, I do not take any sides in the surrounding discussions. Much rather, I hope to use this unique case of a large-scale eHealth technology implementation program as a distinctive and noteworthy foundation to examine various drivers why the 'eGK' program in particular and large-scale eHealth programs in general have struggled to be successfully rolled out in the past.

The nature of this thesis is academic. In other words, my intention is to deduce theoretical contributions to the fields of eHealth and information systems research. Any inferred implications for practice, as later discussed, should not be understood as an infringement of the ways the 'eGK' technology implementation project is currently handled.

Finally, this research thesis builds on some of my prior work as a Ph.D. student at the chair of Information Systems and Management, Prof. Daniel Veit, University of Augsburg. Parts have been published in the Proceedings of the 47th Hawaii International Conference on System Sciences (HICSS), IT Adoption, Diffusion and Evaluation in Healthcare track, January 6–9, 2014, Koloa, Hawaii, USA, as well as in the Proceedings of the European Conference on Information Systems (ECIS), June 9–11, 2014, Tel Aviv, Israel.

# Chapter 1
# Introduction

## 1.1 Motivation

The maintenance of one's personal health is in the interests of every human being. A minimum level of health can be regarded as a most basic necessity for a normal life and healthcare can thus be regarded as fundamental for a functioning society. Implementing professional structures around a working healthcare system has therefore long been a key concern for mankind.

In the 19th century, the overall development of society also sped up to the progression of the healthcare industry. In response to the industrialization, healthcare started to become more and more of a political matter. In Germany, along with Bismarck's introduction of social legislation, the statutory health insurance system was established in 1883, which laid the foundation for the German healthcare system of today. Nowadays a multitude of laws regulates the German healthcare market, which is built around many public and private organizations and individuals that are responsible for a healthy and sustainable population.

Besides the strong political motivation, the development of new medicines and the ever-growing public demand for more and better provision of healthcare services have driven the strong growth of the overall healthcare market. In Germany, just as in most other countries, healthcare accounts for a significant proportion of the overall gross domestic product (GDP). This effect is further augmented, as Germany, like many other developed countries, is an aging society subject to low birth rates and higher life expectancy of over 75 years on average. This will likely lead to a constant if not increasing demand for healthcare and caretaking services in the short and medium term. The resulting, changing demographics and dynamics of healthcare provision can only be answered by continued and substantial reform as well as progress of the healthcare market.

One such progress revolves around the field of *eHealth*, also referred to in the information systems literature as *healthcare information technologies*, *health informatics* or *health IS*. eHealth has become an archetype for healthcare reform in

© Springer International Publishing Switzerland 2015
P. Klöcker, *Resistance Behavior to National eHealth Implementation Programs*,
Progress in IS, DOI 10.1007/978-3-319-17828-8_1

countries around the world and constitutes much more than just a doctor's website or a type of information technology equipment used by one of the many stakeholders within the healthcare sector. In fact, eHealth refers to electronic processes and electronic communication supporting medical procedures within doctors' practices or hospitals often involving the use of the Internet. It is thereby key to understand the interactions amongst the stakeholders within the healthcare sector. So-called e-enabled services, i.e. services which utilize information and communication technologies, further enable these interactions. eHealth therefore requires an all-embracing evaluation of the overall interactions between those stakeholders as well as an optimization of their activities.

While different countries have attempted to implement eHealth technologies in various forms, four key attributes observably characterize an impactful eHealth modernization approach. Firstly, the improvement and modernization of eHealth technologies should take the end user of such a technology into account. In fact, one could argue that end users should be given the opportunity to actively take part in the driving of eHealth programs. Secondly, the entire portfolio and not just segments of the healthcare sector's service portfolio should be targeted. Thirdly, the design of an eHealth program should cut across organizational boundaries therefore engaging the entire healthcare sector. Finally, eHealth programs should build on modern technologies therefore allowing for the realization of possible synergies.

With this in mind, governments across the world have taken different approaches to improve treatment efficiency and effectiveness by making use of eHealth technologies. Over the years, they have launched numerous national programs to integrate doctors, hospitals, pharmacies and patients in national eHealth infrastructures as the examples below demonstrate:

The United States of America (U.S.) has in the past taken various measures to roll out information systems (IS) in the healthcare sector, from early clinical decision support systems in the 1970s and 80s to more advanced electronic health record systems (EHR) in the 1990s and 2000s (Ash and Bates 2005; Berner et al. 2005; Kohn et al. 2000). In 2009, as a response to low implementation rates, the Health Information Technology for Economic and Clinical Health Act (HITECH Act) was signed into law to "provide the necessary assistance and technical support to providers, enable coordination and alignment within and among states, establish connectivity to the public health community in case of emergencies, and assure the workforce is properly trained and equipped to be meaningful users of EHR" (HealthIT.gov). As such, more than $20 billion were set aside to create a nationwide eHealth network which would enable doctors and patients to benefit from functions such as electronic health records or health information exchange (HIE).

In 2004, the European Union (EU) first launched the 2004–2012 eHealth Action plan which has since been replaced by the European Union eHealth Action Plan 2012–2020. This stipulates that the EU will support cross-border sharing of eHealth strategies amongst the member states while generally facilitating uptake and ensuring wider deployment of eHealth technologies. It is hoped that these measures will enable physicians to spend more time with their patients and reduce unnecessary administrative tasks, for example through the use of ePrescription and telemonitoring (European Commission 2012a). Investments continue as the European Commission estimates that the global telemedicine market continues to grow despite the economic crisis, with recent figures suggesting an 18 % increase from $9.8 billion in 2010 to $11.6 billion in 2011. Besides, the global mobile health market (mHealth) is expected to grow to €17.5 billion a year by 2017 (European Commission 2012b).

On a national level, the Danish government was one of the first to publish strategy papers on the digitization of the healthcare sector starting as early as 1996. Since then it has invested heavily to have these ideas realized, see the two case studies by Aanestad and Jensen (2011). They have thereby developed a standardized electronic patient record (EPR) that was already widely used in primary healthcare as well as in hospitals by 2011.

More recently, in 2004, the United Kingdom (U.K.) has set up the 'NHS Connecting for Health' as part of the UK Department of Health with the responsibility of moving England towards central electronic healthcare. One key eHealth function therefore is the National Care Record Service (NCRS) as part of which patients' NHS records are transformed into centrally stored summary care records (SCR). The latter can be accessed by physicians in case of emergency and unscheduled care situations (Currie 2012; Greenhalgh et al. 2008). The introduction of this U.K. program has in the past been referred to as the 'biggest computer program in the world' with alleged costs of over $6 billion and has therefore also been subject of long-standing academic debate (Brennan 2007; Clegg and Shepherd 2007; Currie and Finnegan 2011; Currie and Guah 2007; Currie 2012; Greenhalgh et al. 2008, 2010).

Finally, over the past ten years Germany has taken considerable measures to introduce a national, standardized eHealth system for all health providers. A suitable framework was established with the introduction of a law to modernize the public health insurance system in 2004. In order to digitize the German healthcare sector the 'gematik' (Gesellschaft für Telematikanwendungen der Gesundheitskarte mbh), an organization responsible for the introduction of this national eHealth program, was founded. The rollout process continues at the time of writing. The actual electronic health card ('eGK') has been given to the insured and the infrastructure to be installed at the doctors' and dentists' practices as well as hospitals has partially been distributed. The process of connecting those practices and hospitals online is currently ongoing. According to recent plans, by 2016 the technology will support the function of managing the patient's so-called master data (Versichertenstammdaten—'VSDM') followed by further medical functions in the years to come (please refer to Chap. 2 for a more detailed description of the technology, the rollout process and the stakeholders involved in this process).

Since none of these technologies have been implemented without considerable effort and hence offer a source for research-worthy investigation, it seems paradoxical that academic publications on the topic of eHealth have been scarce until the recent past. This holds true especially in light of the immense everyday relevance of eHealth technologies both in terms of their functional potential as well as their economic significance in relation to countries' spending (Chiasson and

Davidson 2004). Over the last years, however, academic researchers have paid increasing attention to the substantial practical changes involved with eHealth implementation. Agarwal et al. (2010) and Anderson and Agarwal (2011) have highlighted the importance of research on eHealth technologies as it should mirror the many practical changes occurring in this field. They have therefore stressed the need for conducting additional related academic research.

More recently, Romanow et al. (2012) have re-emphasized the standing of eHealth within the overall information systems literature. Moreover, the authors have also stressed the importance of examining user resistance to those eHealth technologies. The phenomenon of user resistance appears highly relevant considering that eHealth implementation programs across the world have often been drawn-out, costly and dispersed as they try to align multiple, powerful stakeholders' preferences. Bhattacherjee and Hikmet (2007) and Lapointe and Rivard (2005) offer recent analyses on user resistance within the eHealth context, discussing it as a result of changing working procedures over which doctors perceive a loss of control as well as in terms of individual and group dynamics.

Indeed, user resistance to eHealth technology might appear less surprising seeing that doctors in most countries have traditionally benefitted from great freedom in how they conduct their work (Walter and Lopez 2008). As new eHealth technologies are introduced, healthcare practitioners are required to alter their working processes. Furthermore, they often have to integrate technologies which either the hospital management, payor institutions or the government force upon them. As a result, especially in the healthcare sector, there has been considerable resistance to replacing manual working practices by information systems technology, a development otherwise discussed as process virtualization (Avison and Young 2007; Barth and Veit 2011; Overby 2008).

## 1.2  Research Questions

This research thesis focuses on the case of the German 'eGK' technology. It is a particularly emotive one, as the introduction of this technology has been strongly opposed by medical doctors and related institutions for more than ten years. The struggle to introduce the 'eGK' technology continues at the time of writing as overall costs for the project have exceeded €1 billion without the functional and technical features in place.

The Oxford English Dictionary defines resistance as the action of resisting, i.e. withstanding an action or effect and trying to prevent it by action or argument. The relevant literature in the fields of information systems respectively eHealth applies varying definitions of user resistance to information systems. Lapointe and Rivard (2005) offer a comprehensive point of view and employ a semantic analysis to summarize these definitions. The authors name five common themes of the concept, which can be used as a basic definition: resistance behavior, object of resistance, perceived threats, initial conditions, and subject of resistance.

Besides, the authors of some of the most influential conceptual studies on user resistance (please see Sect. 3.1) analyze a number of antecedents leading to resistance. These include: one's own feeling of a loss of power, feelings of resentment due to the introduction of a new information system or the influence of colleague opinion. Noticeably, these factors concern either the individual user itself or the user's perceived organizational climate.

In the first instance, this research therefore tries to answer:

*Research Question 1: Is the case of the introduction of the 'eGK' technology one of user resistance theory and do previously developed antecedents appropriately explain user resistance in the context of the 'eGK' technology?*

Strikingly, the above-mentioned antecedents to user resistance are usually factors internal to the organization. Antecedents concerning the wider socio-political and inter-organizational environment, i.e. the user's perceived societal climate, have only marginally been accounted for in the relevant academic literature. However, when looking at the implementation of national IS programs, such as large-scale eHealth programs, it has previously been suggested that one should not ignore the influence of such perceived societal forces on individual user behavior (Currie and Guah 2007; Currie 2012).

In the relevant IS literature perceived societal forces have been explained through the concept of *isomorphic forces* which are often defined as *coercive*, *mimetic* and *normative forces* (Currie 2012; DiMaggio and Powell 1983; Mignerat and Rivard 2012).

Coercive force is formal and informal pressure exerted on organizations by other organizations on which they are dependent as well as by cultural expectations in the society within which this organization functions (DiMaggio and Powell 1983). Within the healthcare sector the regulating government amongst other players can exert coercive force by pushing for the national rollout of eHealth technologies through setting strict deadlines (Jensen et al. 2009).

Mimetic force is defined as the tendency to imitate the actions of structurally equal organizations perceived as successful. In the context of eHealth implementation, mimetic force has been considered a powerful force as medical doctors can feel a strong need to have best practice treatment or latest-standard technology installed within their practice. This is particularly true when they face high uncertainty in terms of the political background and the practical implementation of often highly complex eHealth infrastructures (Currie 2012).

Normative force has been referred to as "members of an organizational field such as suppliers, customers, consultants, and the government … shaping institutional norms regarding implementation and consequent assimilation of [IS] systems" (Liang et al. 2007, p. 66). Jensen et al. (2009) describe normative forces in the context of eHealth as technological trends which doctors will follow for compliance reasons.

Mignerat and Rivard (2012) and Daniels et al. (2002) argue that societal forces, such as isomorphic forces, influence an individual's behavior. This line of argument is of particular importance to this research given that the ultimate users of eHealth technologies are not the government or hospital management, although often responsible for the rollout. In fact the users are the individual doctors, be it in their own practice or within a hospital. "It is therefore important to examine the content of institutional logics, by investigating the specific belief systems as they are understood and interpreted by field members" (Currie and Guah 2007, p. 237; Scott 2001).

Failure to account for the influence of perceived isomorphic forces can result in adverse reaction amongst users. Oliver (1991) discusses how firms engage in defensive action as a result of enforced isomorphic pressure while Currie and Guah (2007) argue that doctors perceive their key task as treating patients not performing administrative tasks. New eHealth technologies, which require them to increasingly do the latter, might not fit their self-perceived professional role hence leading to user resistance. In a second instance this thesis is therefore concerned with answering:

*Research Question 2*: *Which factors, especially with respect to the perceived societal environment, help to further explain user resistance to eHealth technologies amongst physicians?*

A specific focus is thereby laid on examining how perceived societal forces influence individual physicians' behavior and whether these forces can actually move them from resisting to accepting new eHealth technologies. Again, data on the implementation of the 'eGK' technology in Germany is analyzed to answer this second research question.

## 1.3 Research Approach, Methodology and Design

To examine the case of the implementation of the 'eGK' technology in Germany this thesis takes a mixed method approach. *Mixed method research* can be described as the third methodological paradigm given that *quantitative* and *qualitative* research are normally considered the first and second paradigms (Ridenour and Newman 2008; Tashakkori and Teddlie 2003; Venkatesh et al. 2013). Although there has been some debate around whether it is applicable to combine such research methodologics, given that they often rely on very different paradigmatic assumptions, research has suggested that it is appropriate to combine multiple methodologies in so-called *peaceful coexistence*, as suggested for example by Datta (1994) or Rossi (1994), as well as for reasons of triangulation of data, as discussed by Jick (1979), Mingers (2001) and Reichardt and Rallis (1994). In their guideline on how to effectively conduct mixed method research Venkatesh et al. (2013, p. 22) have recently pointed to the need for further studies leveraging mixed methods given that "although the current state of methodological diversity in IS research is encouraging, there is a dearth of research in IS that employs a mixed methods approach".

Mixed method research involves a research design which builds on more than just one research method or alternatively more than one worldview, i.e. qualitative or quantitative research, within a given research inquiry (Tashakkori and Teddlie

2003; Venkatesh et al. 2013). In other words, a mixed method study incorporates both a qualitative and a quantitative research approach. Tashakkori and Teddlie (2003) describe two conceptual ways of combining types of data: *multimethod* and *mixed* methods. In the first approach the researcher makes use of two or more research methods but takes a single worldview, i.e. the researcher may engage in two types of qualitative research, such as an ethnographic study and an additional case study. In the second approach the researcher makes use of both qualitative and quantitative data which she collects either collectively or sequentially. It can therefore be deduced that all mixed method studies are also multimethod studies, but not all multimethod studies are mixed method studies.

Venkatesh et al. (2013) point to three particular strengths of mixed method studies: their ability to simultaneously address exploratory research (normally through qualitative studies) and confirmatory research (normally through quantitative studies), their ability to deliver stronger inferences than a single worldview would often do, and finally their ability to provide the opportunity for a wider angle of different and/or complementary views. Mixed methods research is therefore considered to be particularly strong with regards to explaining complex organizational and social phenomena and an increasing number of authors have called for IS researchers to conduct research which employs mixed methods (Cao et al. 2006; Mingers 2001; Venkatesh et al. 2013).

This study aims to shed light on the highly complex nature of national eHealth implementation programs involving numerous stakeholders subject to personal characteristics, multifaceted organizational environments as well as diverse perceived isomorphic forces. Given the complex nature of the subject of the study, taking a mixed method approach appears to be particularly appropriate.

Overall therefore, this thesis follows the approach to conducting mixed methods research described by Venkatesh et al. (2013). The authors suggest that every mixed method study should fulfill the following three criteria: (1) the appropriateness of the mixed method approach has to be ensured; (2) meta-inference can be developed from the data; (3) the quality of the meta-inference can be assessed, i.e. validity of the data is ensured. In other words, they respectively offer a guideline on when to employ mixed methods research, how to uncover and develop possible integrative findings from the mixed methods research and finally how to assess the quality of these findings.

## *1.3.1 Strategy for Conducting Mixed Method Research*

Depending on the event under study Venkatesh et al. (2013) suggest several strategies to be pursued when conducting mixed method research. The authors also divide the purpose of a mixed method study into seven categories. For example, if the goal of a study is to understand the event as it occurs (i.e. the development or implementation of new software), a so-called *concurrent* mixed methods design approach should be used. If, however, the objective of a research inquiry is to better understand the reaction of the users of that new technology, a researcher should take a so-called *sequential* approach. The researcher could thereby use interviews to develop a core set of antecedents leading to the users' reactions and then develop and test a theory from these.

Taking this into account this thesis is built around a sequential rather than a concurrent mixed method research design. As such, qualitative data was collected and analyzed before a main quantitative study was conducted (please refer to Table 1.1 as well as Fig. 1.1). Creswell (2003) suggest that this is appropriate when qualitative data is used for exploratory purposes and the results are later tested in a large quantitative study for generalizability to a certain population.

**Table 1.1** Purpose and nature of mixed method approach adapted from Venkatesh et al. (2013)

| Purpose of study | Characteristics | Authors' comments |
|---|---|---|
| Purpose of mixed method approach | 'Developmental' | A quantitative pilot study tested the appropriateness of user resistance theory to the thesis' practical context, while qualitative study helped identify a set of tangible variables from which appropriate hypotheses could be developed |
| Nature of mixed method approach | Sequential approach: informative, less dominant studies (quantitative pilot study as well as qualitative study) followed by dominant quantitative study | Although extensive qualitative data was gathered it was mainly used for the exploratory purpose of identifying a set of tangible variables which were subsequently tested in the main quantitative study |

**Fig. 1.1** Outline of mixed method approach in three phases

Furthermore, this research takes a *developmental* purpose (please also refer to Table 1.1). According to Venkatesh et al. (2013, p. 26) a developmental, sequential design can be used if "one strand provides hypotheses to be tested in the next one". Indeed, such an approach has not been uncommon in the field of information systems research (Becerra-Fernandez and Sabherwal 2001; Grimsley and Meehan 2007; Ho et al. 2003).

## 1.3.2   Data Analysis

In terms of the analysis of the data, Venkatesh et al. (2013) go on to suggest that the dominant study in the overall research is characterized by particularly rigorous data collection and analysis. On the contrary, less detail about the data collection process and analysis is provided for the non-dominant study. In this research thesis, the dominant study is the final quantitative study while the less dominant studies are the exploratory qualitative study and the quantitative pilot study. Nonetheless, as later described, the non-dominant studies were also examined for their validity according to the rigorous standards suggested by relevant research in the field of study.

## 1.3.3   Development of Meta-inference

Venkatesh et al. (2013, p. 38) define *meta-inference* as the "theoretical statements, narratives, or a story inferred from an integration of findings from quantitative and qualitative strands of mixed methods research." The authors list three possible ways of obtaining meta-inference from mixed methods research: firstly, merging of qualitative and quantitative findings, secondly use of quantitative findings and then qualitative findings, finally, use of qualitative findings and then quantitative findings.

Once a research has embarked on one of these three paths they can then choose between so-called *bracketing* and *bridging* to develop meta-inference (Lewis and Grimes 1999). Bracketing describes the process of incorporating diverse and/or opposing views about the phenomenon observed. Bridging describes the process of developing a consensus from the qualitative and quantitative data obtained.

This research thesis is conducted in three phases (see Fig. 1.1) leveraging extensive data collected on the 'eGK' technology implementation project. In the first phase, a set of quantitative data from an online questionnaire distributed to physicians in Germany is leveraged to conduct a pilot study. It is verified whether user resistance theory is an applicable theory in the context of eHealth as suggested both by the relevant literature and the practical motivation around the case of implementation of the German 'eGK' technology. The pilot study builds on the existing 'Status Quo Bias Model' by Kim and Kankanhalli (2009) empirically testing and validating the relevant constructs.

In the second phase extensive qualitative data is used to identify and isolate other factors since they have previously been suggested to play an important role in shaping eHealth implementation programs, namely isomorphic, societal forces. These are categorized according to the stakeholders involved in the implementation of the 'eGK' technology.

Finally, in the third phase the influence of these perceived isomorphic forces on individual physician's behavior is empirically tested. For this purpose a large quantitative data set is collected via an online survey distributed to German physicians who will be provided with the 'eGK' technology.

### 1.3.4 Assessment of Meta-inference

Finally, Venkatesh et al. (2013) make explicit that researchers need to ensure that both the design and execution of the qualitative and quantitative studies follow the norms and expectations of the overall research field. Besides, the researchers should employ a rigorous strategy for the integration of the findings from both the quantitative and qualitative data. Only then will the studies provide accurate meta-inferences with powerful and high-quality insights.

The following Table 1.2 summarizes the guidelines for conducting mixed method research as suggested by Venkatesh et al. (2013) and furthermore provides an overview on how they are addressed in this thesis.

## 1.4  Outline

The thesis is organized as follows: first, the reader is given a comprehensive overview of the German healthcare market, its development over the past years as well as its peculiar characteristics compared to other healthcare markets around the world. Particular focus is put on describing the introduction of the German electronic health card, 'eGK', and the many controversies surrounding it. This is outlined in Chap. 2.

Next, in Chap. 3, the relevant literature in the field of eHealth within the information systems literature is discussed, in particular relevant contributions on user resistance and stakeholder behavior in the field of eHealth. Sections 3.1 and 3.3 take a step back and examine the more general theoretical works both on user resistance theory and on theory surrounding isomorphic pressures within the information systems literature.

Given the mixed method approach to collecting data used on this topic, the thesis is then split into three phases (please refer to Fig. 1.1): Phase I, i.e. Chap. 4 describes the pilot study conducted in order to test the 'Status Quo Bias Model' in the context of the 'eGK' technology. The hypotheses of the model, the data

**Table 1.2** Mixed method approach and guidelines

| Quality aspects | Quality criteria | Authors' response to Venkatesh et al.'s guideline |
|---|---|---|
| Purpose of mixed method approach | 'Development' | • This study is divided in three phases leveraging, (1) a small quantitative study, (2) qualitative interviews along with extensive documentary analysis and participant observations as part of an exploratory case study and (3) a large quantitative survey<br>• This strategy of first testing for the appropriateness of resistance theory to the research problem, then examining raw data from the phenomenon to identify further relevant drivers of user behavior and finally measuring these in a larger quantitative study ensured that the research model tested in the final quantitative study was relevant to the phenomenon of interest (Yin 1993)<br>• In doing so this study combines the advantages of both a qualitative and a quantitative approach. It achieves depth as well as insight into the phenomenon while also allowing for a wider generalizability of the findings |
| Design quality | Design adequacy | *Quantitative*<br>• The final research model was built on a both a smaller quantitative study as well as a theory-driven exploratory case study, suggesting factors to be empirically tested in the final model<br>• The constructs measured were mainly well established scales<br>• Rounds of items sorting were performed<br>• The validity of instruments was assessed<br>• An appropriate sampling frame and sample size were chosen |
| | | *Qualitative*<br>• *Selecting suitable interview partners*: The interview partners were suitably chosen: (a) due to their yearlong expert knowledge on the subject of study; (b) so that at least one representative from each of the relevant stakeholder groups involved in the rollout of the eHealth technology was interviewed (government official, 'gematik', umbrella organizations of both payors and providers, individual doctors, external consultants)<br>• *Entering the field with credibility*: Contact was established through an official e-mail from the university chair introducing the research and researchers to potential interviewees. This both lead to snowballing and theoretical sampling effects opening doors to further interview partners, while also ensuring a representative sample |

(continued)

**Table 1.2** (continued)

| Quality aspects | Quality criteria | Authors' response to Venkatesh et al.'s guideline |
|---|---|---|
| | | • *Conduct of interviews*: Semi-structured interviews were conducted partially voice-recorded, partially based on protocol. The interviewers were furthermore sensitive to the principles of flexibility, non-direction, specificity and range (Flick 1998) |
| | Analytical adequacy | *Quantitative*<br>• Justification of the choice of the analysis technique (PLS)<br>• Sample size of 469 ensured meaningful analysis<br>• Data was professionally collected ensuring that bias in the sampling of subjects was minimized (employment of specialized data/research firm) |
| | | *Qualitative*<br>• The data was triangulated in terms of Data, Methodology and Investigator providing substantiation of constructs and hypotheses (Eisenhardt 1989; Patton 2002)<br>• Semi-structured interviews were conducted in order to allow interviewees to elaborate according to their experience. The interview process stopped at point of saturation of information<br>• Skepticism with regards to the interview data was maintained in line with the principle of suspicion (Klein and Myers 1999)<br>• Key themes are illustrated making use of quotations to enhance plausibility<br>• Although the notion of inter-rater reliability was not employed, the researchers involved in the data collection procedure identified key concepts in consensus, suggesting some form of convergence and/or reliability<br>• Given the exploratory nature of the study aimed at discovering new themes by making use of raw data, the notion of theoretical validity is not applicable to this case |
| Explanation quality | Quantitative inference | • *Internal validity*: a theoretically robust model was developed, control variables were employed, reliability of the data collection process and measurements was ensured, appropriate statistical tests were performed<br>• *Statistical conclusion validity* (further case of internal validity): the reliability and the validity of the measurement model were ensured, the structural model was assessed, an appropriate level of significance for tests was assumed, the common method variance was appropriately tested [i.e., through Harman's single-factor test (Podsakoff et al. 2003)]<br>• *External validity*: 469 German physicians represent a significant proportion of German doctors provided |

(continued)

**Table 1.2** (continued)

| Quality aspects | Quality criteria | Authors' response to Venkatesh et al.'s guideline |
|---|---|---|
| | | with the 'eGK' technology. Potential bias in sampling was minimized by employing a research firm specialized in the healthcare sector to provide a representative sample of physicians to whom the online questionnaire was sent |
| | Qualitative inference | • The constructs identified in the qualitative study were plausible as also suggested by a systematic review of the relevant literature<br>• The constructs were proven relevant in the quantitative survey of 469 German physicians |
| | Integrative inference | • *Integrative efficacy*: Thanks to the exploratory case study, which offered an extensive, real-life perspective on the phenomenon, original antecedents for the various perceived isomorphic forces by stakeholder could be deduced. Many of these loaded significantly. At the same time, an $R^2$ of 35 % suggests a good balance between close analysis and overall fit. This synergy between the two studies provides evidence for a satisfactory level of integrative efficacy<br>• *Inference transferability*: The set of antecedents derived from the mixed method research can and should be tested in other contexts where isomorphic pressures are applicably perceived<br>• *Integrative correspondence*: The meta-interference of the mixed method study, whereby the exploratory qualitative data offered a suitable basis for the quantitative study, therefore also satisfied the initial 'developmental' purpose of the overall research |

*Note* Adapted from Venkatesh et al. (2013)

collection procedure and the analysis of this data are discussed in Sects. 4.2 and 4.3 respectively. Finally, the results are reviewed in Sect. 4.4.

Phase II, i.e. Chap. 5, describes the collection and analysis of qualitative data obtained from insights on the 'eGK' technology implementation project as well as interviews with relevant stakeholders. Subsequently, the results of the data analysis are reviewed and various forces that drive user resistance to eHealth technologies are deduced.

Phase III, i.e. Chap. 6, builds upon these findings taking the key results as a basis for developing a specific theoretical model on user resistance to the 'eGK' technology. The model is tested using a large quantitative data set. Again, the hypotheses behind the model are thoroughly described. A detailed description of standard statistical data analysis techniques is provided before the concrete research methodology including a description of the sample, the data collection procedure and the analysis of this data are explained in Sects. 6.2–6.5. Section 6.6 concludes with a discussion of the findings from this quantitative study.

Finally, in Chap. 7, the theoretical and practical contributions of the overall research as well as possible limitations of this study are presented. The thesis concludes with Chap. 8.

# Chapter 2
# Contextual Background

## 2.1 A Brief Outline of the Historical Development of eHealth Technologies

Before looking more closely at how Germany's healthcare system works, analyzing what the introduction of the 'eGK' technology in Germany entails and who is responsible for its rollout, this subsection provides a brief overview of the development of eHealth technologies over the past years.

Within the field of eHealth the term telemedicine has in the past been used to describe the "delivery of health care and the exchange of healthcare-information across distance" encompassing "the whole range of medical activities including diagnosis, treatment and prevention of disease, continuing education of health-care providers and consumers, and research and evaluation" (Craig and Patterson 2005, p. 3). Quite possibly the earliest form of eHealth was the use of telemedicine in the form of bonfires to pass on information about the bubonic plague across countries back in the Middle Ages. These forms of messaging have since been continuously developed, first with the rise of postal services, then telegraphy in the mid-19th century, which were eventually replaced by the telephone, and finally the radio.

Thanks to substantive technological development modern telemedicine has evolved away from analogue techniques towards digital forms of communication. Today, services using television, teleconferencing devices or the Internet can be considered a quasi-standard in practices and hospitals across developed countries. In fact, there often is no alternative to using telemedicine these days. By connecting the most remote locations telemedicine allows for better healthcare provision across countries thereby also improving the overall integration of healthcare providers and patients (Craig and Patterson 2005).

More recently, the term eHealth has been introduced to encompass not only telemedicine but add a broader dimension to "an emerging field in the intersection of medical informatics, public health and business, referring to health services and information delivered or enhanced through the Internet and related

© Springer International Publishing Switzerland 2015
P. Klöcker, *Resistance Behavior to National eHealth Implementation Programs*,
Progress in IS, DOI 10.1007/978-3-319-17828-8_2

technologies"(Eysenbach 2001). The expression of eHealth has therefore been labeled as the "death of telemedicine because—in the context of a broad availability of medical information systems that can interconnect and communicate—telemedicine will no longer exist as a specific field" (Della Mea 2001).

In Germany, eHealth technologies have been employed for years. In the form of telemedicine the so-called Telemedical Maritime Assistance Service (TMAS) dates back to the early 1930s. In the 1970s in-house emergency call services were increasingly introduced, while in the 1990s retirement homes across the country were equipped with broadband video-communication (Paulus and Romanowski 2009).

The demand for a centralized eHealth technology with functionality beyond pure telemedical communication gained momentum with the so-called "Lipobay scandal" in 2001. The pharmaceutical company, Bayer, was forced to withdraw their medication, Lipobay/Baycol, as it showed severe side effects especially in combination with other subscribed medication (Die Zeit 2002). Due to the lack of electronic patient files these side effects were also hard to trace. A subsequent study published by the consulting firm Roland Berger therefore called for the need for a chip-based health card that would be able store such information (please refer to Sects. 2.5 and 2.6 for a further description of the development of the 'eGK' technology).

## 2.2 Healthcare in Germany

Germany offers a national healthcare system, wherein every citizen of the state must be either nationally (statutorily) or privately insured. As of 01st January 2014 approximately 70 million of the 82 million German citizens are members of one of 132 statutory health insurance companies (GKV-Spitzenverband). As such, they are entitled by law to receive treatment in order to maintain and restore their personal health according to a catalogue which is collectively agreed upon by payors, providers and the government.

The Ministry of Health assumes the governing body for the healthcare sector and is responsible for all national matters with regards to health, prevention and long-term care. It also regulates European and international health tasks. The provision and financing of public healthcare services is done through self-governing institutions. These are amongst others the statutory health insurance companies and associations of medical doctors. In 2012, expenditure in the healthcare sector was ca. €300 billion which resulted mainly from expenditure of the statutory and private health insurance companies, expenditure of private households and organizations without commercial interest as well as goods and services which were provided in the context of ambulant treatments. This amount corresponds to approximately 11.3 % of the German gross domestic product (Statistisches Bundesamt 2014).

The statutory health insurance system is financed by the statutory health insurance funds. These are public-law corporations and are both financially and organizationally independent. While being assigned tasks by the state, these corporations carry out their tasks on their own responsibility. The statutory health insurance system is based on the principles of solidarity and benefits in kind. The solidarity principle ensures that each insured person receives the medically necessary benefits regardless of their income. The principle of benefits in kind warrants benefits without the patient having to make up-front payments.

As of January 2009, the statutory health insurance benefits are funded through a national Health Fund based on a uniform contribution rate for all insured citizens. Both employers and employees pay parts of the contributions into this fund via the statutory health insurance.

Thus, while other countries introducing eHealth technologies have tax-financed systems, i.e. the U.K., Germany's overall statutory healthcare system is financed through contributions. The German system also differs considerably from the somewhat mixed system in the U.S. where healthcare provision, for example through the so-called 'medicare' and 'medicaid' systems, can be both provision- and tax-financed.

Importantly, in Germany doctors are not employees of the government or specific payor institutions, unlike in other countries such as the U.K. They therefore have a constitutionally ensured scope for discretion with respect to choosing the appropriate therapy as well as to voicing their opinion towards changes in the system. On the one hand, the German system thus allows providers, payors and patients great liberties in the overall provision and claiming of healthcare services respectively. On the other hand, this set-up adds stakeholder complexity as in the case of the 'eGK' technology whereby payors and providers generally act independently of the government and of one another. As such, each party individually has to be convinced of the benefits of new eHealth systems. Indeed, each stakeholder group aims at maximizing their own utility as the 'eGK' technology implementation project continues.

## 2.3 The Reasons for Introducing the 'eGK' in Germany

While the so-called "Lipobay scandal" in 2001 is often cited as being the catalyst for why the rollout of a central eHealth system including electronic patient files were demanded, it should be noted that the reasons for introducing the 'eGK' technology are manifold. Indeed, different stakeholders involved in the process are to benefit from the advantages of the 'eGK' technology in different ways and to a different extent. Some of the most prominent advantages can be summarized as follows:

Firstly, there is a general transformation favoring digital technologies in both the public and the private sector that has already penetrated the healthcare industry to a considerable extent. Indeed, countrywide eHealth systems are no longer the exception (please refer to Sect. 3.2 for a detailed discussion of the relevant literature on other national eHealth systems) while patient-focused technologies, such as medical mobile applications, are also increasingly being developed around the world. These eHealth technologies generate substantial overall economic and technological benefits to patients, doctors and the medical technology industry alike. With its 'eGK' technology Germany logically follows this trend.

Secondly, two major cost-benefit analyses commissioned in 2006 and 2011 have suggested that there is a considerable economic benefit associated with the introduction of the 'eGK' technology (Gesellschaft für Telematikanwendungen der Gesundheitskarte mbh and Booz Allen Hamilton 2006). According to these reports, the 'eGK' technology directly profits both the insurance companies and therefore also the insurant who arguably pay unnecessarily high insurance contributions. The 'eGK' may therefore reduce the administrative costs of giving out new cards, for example when an insured person changes their insurance status. Furthermore, with a picture of the insurant printed on the card the insurance companies hope to avoid a considerable amount of fraud whereby an artificer of such fraud would illegally use a stolen insurance card.

Lastly and probably most importantly, a lot of qualitative benefits come along with the 'eGK' technology, the value of which goes beyond a simple measurement in monetary terms. Notably patients stand to gain from these qualitative benefits, i.e. medical functions of the 'eGK' technology, that are said to enable doctors to deliver more effective and efficient treatment, as explained later in this section.

## 2.4  Key Stakeholders in the 'eGK' Implementation Project

### 2.4.1  The Health Insurance Companies (Payors)

As mentioned above German citizens can choose amongst 132 statutory healthcare insurance companies whereby healthcare insurance is mandatory for every citizen of the state (GKV-Spitzenverband). Both the citizen and her employer normally pay the insurance contribution. Above a certain annual income threshold a citizen has the option of joining one of the private insurance companies.

In the context of the 'eGK' technology implementation the insurance companies are generally referred to as 'payors' ('Kostenträger') given that they are paying for the whole of the implementation process including the funding of the 'gematik' (definition below) as well as the rollout and subsequent maintenance of the hard- and software to be installed in the doctors' medical practices.

While various healthcare and care insurance companies have employees dedicated to the work on the implementation of the 'eGK' technology, they are also centrally represented by an umbrella organization in this matter (Spitzenverband der Gesetzlichen Krankenversicherungen, 'GKV-SV'). The GKV-SV was founded as part of the law § 217a SGB V in 2007. Overall, it determines general conditions for competitiveness within the health insurance market, both in terms of economic feasibility and the quality of the insurance services provided. It also supports the healthcare insurance providers in terms of meeting their responsibilities and in terms of the representation of their interests. One example of this is their assistance in developing a system for standardized electronic data transmission amongst all statutory insurance providers. The GKV-SV generally supports the introduction of the 'eGK' and represents the interests of the statutory insurance companies within the 'gematik'.

## 2.4.2 The Doctors (Providers)

As of 2011, approximately 342,000 doctors practice medical services in Germany. The largest categories of specialization are: 101,000 general practitioners, 101,000 doctors for general, internal and child medicine as well as 36,000 surgeons and orthopedic surgeons. Additionally, 69,000 dentists, 36,000 psychotherapists and 61,000 pharmacists work in Germany (Statistisches Bundesamt 2013a). In 2012, 2017 hospitals operated across the country (Statistisches Bundesamt 2013b).

In the context of implementing the 'eGK' technology the doctors are often referred to as 'providers' ('Leistungserbringer') given that they will be the ones using the 'eGK' technology on a daily basis while providing medical services to their patients.

Overall, all resident doctors no matter their specialization, all hospitals and all dentists will eventually be provided with the 'eGK' technology according to current rollout plans. Furthermore, the 'eGK' technology is also intended to connect pharmacies across the country making use of specific functions such as the ePrescription ('eRezept'), whereby a prescription is electronically wired from doctor to pharmacy.

Within the 'gematik' the interests of the various providers are represented by the German Medical Association (Bundesärztekammer—'BÄK'), the German Dental Association (Bundeszahnärztekammer—'BZÄK'), the German Pharmacists' Association (Deutscher Apothekerverband e.V.—'DAV'), the German Hospital Federation (Deutsche Krankenhausgesellschaft—'DKG'), the National Association of Statutory Health Insurance Physicians (Kassenärztliche Bundesvereinigung —'KBV') and the National Association of Statutory Health Insurance Dentists (Kassenzahnärztliche Bundesvereinigung—'KZBV'). These organizations are all, just like the GKV-SV, direct shareholders in the 'gematik'.

## 2.4.3 The 'Gematik'

In 2002, the lead associations of both payors (health insurers) and providers (doctors) decided to collaborate on the implementation of the 'eGK' technology, which was anchored in the German law to modernize the public German health insurance system (§ 291 (2a) SGB V) in 2004.

In particular, § 291a and § 291b regulate that the conceptual and operational realization of this eHealth program is to be carried out by the Society for Telematics Applications (Gesellschaft für Telematikanwendungen der Gesundheitskarte mbH

—'gematik'), which was founded in January 2005 as a special purpose vehicle for this task. The organizational structure and governance is described in law § 291a (7) Sentence 1, SGB V and lists the shareholders as mentioned above. The 'gematik' is primarily responsible for the specification and certification of the various technical and systemic parts to be installed at doctors' practices, hospitals and in the backbone. The 'gematik' has approximately 180 employees in Berlin (Gesellschaft für Telematikanwendungen der Gesundheitskarte mbh).

The 'gematik' is governed to equal parts by both the lead associations of payors and providers, who hold 50 % of the shares respectively. Decision-making is regulated by law and requires 67 % of the votes in a shareholders' meeting.

Until 01st July 2009 both the statutory and private health insurance companies were involved in the planning and implementation process of the 'eGK' technology. However, as of July 2009 the private insurance companies have withdrawn from the 'gematik' and have handed over their share to the statutory insurance companies to keep the 50 and 50 % balance in shares between payors and providers. This move therefore means that privately insured citizens are not given the 'eGK' for the time being. As long as this remains the case, these patients will also not be able to access their medical data electronically over the countrywide 'eGK' system.

### 2.4.4 The Federal Ministry of Health

The 'eGK' implementation project was essentially started by the Federal Ministry of Health (Bundesministerium für Gesundheit—'BMG'), which was headed by the Social Democratic Party of Germany (Sozialdemokratische Partei Deutschlands —'SPD') and the Green Party (BÜNDNIS 90/DIE GRÜNEN) at the time this decision was made. Already in 2003, the BMG contracted a number of companies to form the so-called 'bIT4health', a consortium commissioned to determine the general requirements for introducing a nationwide eHealth infrastructure in Germany. In 2004, the BMG subsequently introduced the law to modernize the public German health insurance system, § 291 SGB V. In 2005, it furthermore published an act which regulates the regional testing procedures required prior to the full, nationwide rollout of the 'eGK' technology (Verordnung über Testmaßnahmen für die Einführung der elektronischen Gesundheitskarte). Until today, the BMG remains closely involved in the project.

### 2.4.5 The Federal Office for Information Security and Federal Commissioner for Data Protection and Freedom of Information

Overall, the German government as well as the key stakeholders responsible for the implementation of the 'eGK' technology have gone to great lengths to ensure a high standard of data security. Apart from the Federal Ministry of Health, both the Federal Office for Information Security (Bundesamt für Sicherheit in der Informationstechnik—'BSI') and Federal Commissioner for Data Protection and Freedom of Information (Bundesbeauftragte für den Datenschutz und die Informationsfreiheit—'BfDI) are heavily involved in the realization of this eHealth program. The 'gematik' reports closely and directly on the technical specifications of the various technological components as well as the data transmission process as a whole.

The BSI, in charge of data security, has issued clear guidelines for the technological specifications of the 'eGK' infrastructure. They are expressed in so-called protection profiles and set the standard for the required data security. As such, these standards affect the configuration of, for example, the key components of the Connector or the card reading terminals (definitions in Sect. 2.5).

In the past, the BfDI, responsible for data privacy, has been critical of the old health insurance cards (Krankenversicherungskarte—'KVK') for containing patients' master data in an unprotected form. It has therefore voiced its general consent to the 'eGK' technology while nonetheless underlining the importance of establishing a truly safe connection of the doctors' medical practices. The BfDI has furthermore recognized that one important benefit of the new technological standard is the introduction of a standardized form of logging. The new 'eGK' technology thus allows for informing the patients about which personal data is read and updated on the 'eGK'.

## 2.4.6 The Medical Technology Industry

Over the years a significant number of technology providers have been involved in the development of the various technological components for the envisioned 'eGK' technology. Companies have focused on and specialized on developing individual products and services, such as the connector, the card reading terminal or the provision of a secure Internet connection (see below for definitions). In previous as well as in future tests of the 'eGK' technology, consortia of technology providers have formed to offer a holistic product and service for a test region.

The providers of medical technology produce the components according to the strict functional and technological standards determined by the 'gematik'. The 'gematik' also manages the tendering process for the consortia and is therefore ultimately responsible for selecting the technological solutions employed during the various test phases. In the final rollout physicians will likely be able to acquire the individual components of the 'eGK' technology from various providers who produce these according to the final specifications of the 'gematik'.

## 2.5  The Technology Behind the 'eGK'

Compared to the former health insurance card (Krankenversichertenkarte—'KVK'), the 'eGK' itself has a number of important new features (see Fig. 2.1):

1. The most noticeable, physical change to the new 'eGK' is a picture of the insured person, which is to guard against misuse of the card, i.e. in case of loss or theft.
2. The new health insurance number, which is issued alongside the new card, is retained also in the case where a patient changes her insurance provider.
3. The microchip is used to store the patient's so-called master data (Versichertenstammdaten—'VSDM') in a protected environment. This includes the name, date of birth, address data, insurance number and data on how the patient is ensured, i.e. whether as member or family insurance policy-holder.
4. The name of the card is now standardized.

Figure 2.2 presents a simplified representation of the envisioned 'eGK' technology including its key components:

- *Doctor's personal computer ('PC')*—The doctor's personal computer encompasses the primary system of the practice or hospital, i.e. the relevant medical software. If not already connected to the Internet, the doctor's PC will be connected to the Internet during the rollout of the 'eGK' technology to permit an online transmission of relevant data.
- *Card reading terminal for 'eGK'*—The 'eGK' card reading terminal is a device specifically designed for the insertion and reading of the 'eGK'. It can loosely be compared to a credit card reading device as often used in shops or restaurants and is either directly connected to the Connector (definition below) or works as a mobile device, for example in an ambulance.
- *Card reading terminal for 'HBA'*—Another card reading terminal will be connected to the Connector, which reads the doctor's Health Professional Card (Heilberufsausweis—'HBA'). The HBA is the doctor's own personal ID authorizing her to access a patient's electronic health data.

**Fig. 2.1** Sample picture of the 'eGK'. *Source* 'Kartengrafik: gematik GmbH'

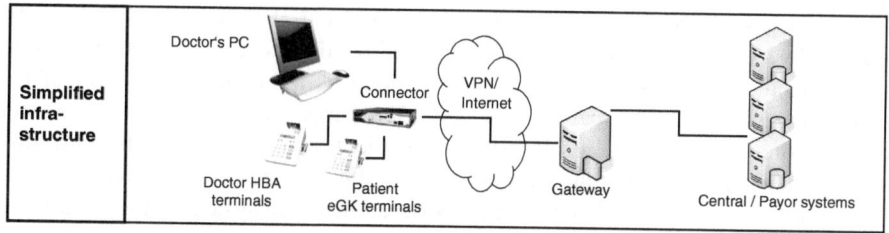

**Fig. 2.2**  Simplified depiction of 'eGK' technology

- *Connector*—The Connector works as an authentication and encryption device while also protecting the doctor's local computer and primary system from the outside, given that it will be connected to the Internet in the future. Effectively, the Connector establishes a safe Virtual private network ('VPN') between the doctor's personal computer and the Gateway (definition below). The Connector includes an application logic, which triggers the data transmission between the 'eGK' and the central/payor systems (definition below) and furthermore ensures the update of any data on the card itself.
- *Network*—The network can be a standard Internet connection as provided by one of the many telecommunications providers in the country. The doctor's medical practice or a hospital can be connected for example via a Digital Subscriber Line ('DSL') or a Universal Mobile Telecommunications System ('UMTS') common in German households. The type of network used will also depend on whether a stationary or mobile device is being connected.
- *Gateway*—The Gateway concentrates the many VPN protected networks arriving from the doctor's medical practices and connects them with the central/payor systems at the back of the system.
- *Central systems*—The Central systems are part of the back-end of the 'eGK' technology and are responsible for the implementation of relevant data safety requirements. These are particularly relevant as in its final version the 'eGK' technology will transmit a large number of highly sensitive personal medical data.
- *Payor systems*—The Payor systems are also part of the back-end of the 'eGK' technology and encompass a number of systems, for example the Update Flag Service ('UFS'), which consolidates the requests for the update of data saved on the 'eGK'.

From a user perspective and taking a non-technical approach, i.e. without listing all technical transmissions between every single component, the 'eGK' technology works as follows: Assuming a patient's standard visit to their general practitioner, the patient's 'eGK' is inserted into the dedicated card reading terminal, which is directly connected to the Connector. The patient enters her personal pin thus authorizing the doctor to access and store her medical data. The Connector is in turn connected to the doctor's personal computer (see Fig. 2.2). A safe Internet connection is established between the doctor's personal computer and the so-called backbone, which consists of the Gateway, the Central systems as well as the insurance companies' Payor systems. The 'eGK' therefore works as the key to retrieving the electronic data from the backbone as it initiates the set-up of the connection between the local and the central systems. While the patient's master data is stored on the 'eGK' itself, no other medical data is stored on the card, first and foremost to avoid it being decoded should the card be lost or stolen.

Key to establishing a safe connection between the local system of the doctor and the backbone is the Connector. It also encrypts all data before it leaves the doctor's office. With this in place, the 'eGK' is first checked to determine whether the patient's master data is up to date. For example, should the patient have changed her address and have reported this change to her insurance company, the insurance company will update their data in the payor system. As the 'eGK' is inserted and a connection is established between the doctor's personal computer and the backbone, the new address is updated and saved on the card. The process of updating the patient's master data is the most basic function of the 'eGK' technology.

Once the 'eGK' technology is fully implemented, the patient's actual medical data can be retrieved and exchanged. For this purpose the doctor has to insert her own HBA at the same time that the 'eGK' is inserted. The HBA works as an authorization device signaling to the Central system that the doctor is accredited to retrieve the patient's highly sensitive medical data ('card-to-card authorization'). It furthermore allows the doctor to electronically enter new medical records.

Apart from being able to transmit the patients master data, the 'eGK' technology will in the future also comprise further key functions, as stated in SGB V § 291a. It is important to notice that according to law the patient alone has the right to decide which data is stored on the card and who is granted access to the medical data. The additional functions, described below, are therefore also referred to as 'voluntary' functions:

- Electronic emergency data (Notfalldaten)—By choice a patient can have relevant information, such as allergies, chronic diseases, drug intolerances as well as other important diagnoses saved on the 'eGK'. Further, the address of a contact person in case of an emergency as well as the contact information of the primary doctor can be stored. In this case, any doctor can access this relevant information even without the patient's immediate consent. This feature is particularly useful when the doctor has to act quickly and the patient is not able to respond. Besides, if so wanted, the patient's provision as well as information on their willingness to donate organs can be saved.
- Electronic doctor letter (eArztbrief /KOM-LE)—Today, doctors mostly communicate via post. One drawback of this is that information can sometimes not be shared on time between two doctors simultaneously treating the same patient. Furthermore, doctors already working with digital patient files also need to transfer the relevant information into the computer system of their medical practice which can be unnecessarily time consuming. The electronic doctor letter allows doctors to quickly share diagnostic findings in a legally binding, safe and compatible manner.

- Data for checking the drug therapy safety (AMTS)—On a voluntary basis, patients can choose to have data on medications, drug prescriptions or suggestions for therapy electronically documented. As such, a doctor or pharmacist can get an overview over the different drugs a patient is taking. A key advantage of this feature is that it should reduce the risk of prescribing or selling drugs which cause interactions with negative consequences.
- Electronic case file (eFallakte)—In the future, all doctors involved in a certain treatment process can be permitted access to the documentation of this treatment case. This data will be saved in the electronic case file and should enable a better harmonization of individual medical cases.
- Electronic patient file (Patientenfach)—This function enables the storage of data provided by the patients themselves.
- Electronic patient receipt (Patientenquittung)—Patients will be able to ask their doctor for a patient receipt which can be issued on the very day of the treatment or on a quarterly basis.

To sum up, while the 'eGK' technology is transforming the use of technology in German medical practices and therefore also the way patients will be treated in the future, it does not require the total dismantlement of currently used hard- and software within the various medical practices and hospitals. This is important to notice and a key difference to other information systems implementations observed in some of the existing literature on eHealth technologies (Aanestad and Jensen 2011; Hanseth and Monteiro 1998). As such, only the interfaces to the doctor's PC and the payor systems will have to be to adjusted to accommodate the use of the 'eGK' technology. Other components such as the card-reading terminals, the Internet connection and most of the backbone infrastructure will be independently developed, installed and configured. Indeed, this is an important prerequisite in order to be able to operate a safe and autonomous system that cannot be breached from the outside. Many of the existing data privacy concerns and corresponding strict regulation could otherwise not be met.

Furthermore, the newly developed and installed components of the 'eGK's' technology are mostly purpose-built. An "adaptability problem", which should, according to Hanseth and Lyytinen (2010), be avoided by making simple, modularized information infrastructures, therefore only partially applies to the 'eGK' technology.

## 2.6 The Implementation Process of the 'eGK' Technology

### 2.6.1 The Implementation Process of the 'eGK' Technology Until Today

Puzzlingly, despite the implementation process of the 'eGK' being clearly regulated by law, despite the set-up of a special-purpose vehicle to steer the process, i.e. the 'gematik', despite the general support of the relevant governmental bodies and despite a general willingness by technology providers to develop and produce the technical components according to the strict specifications, the rollout of the 'eGK' technology has been difficult right from the outset.

Initial plans as stated by law (§ 291 (1) SGB V) envisioned a rollout of the 'eGK' technology by January 2006. However, difficulties were already encountered early on: Technical and functional demands continuously increased as the stakeholders involved in the implementation process struggled to agree on a number of points, amongst them concerns about the functionality of the technology and how it would be used on a daily basis. Further points of disagreement evolved around the timing of the rollout, details on the planned testing procedures and data privacy concerns.

In 2006, the 'gematik' consequently commissioned a cost-benefit analysis of the program, which mapped the costs of the rollout and day-to-day operations of hard- and software against the saving potentials encompassed in the new technology. Savings were therefore calculated to result from avoiding unnecessary administrative costs. These were often associated with the issuing of new cards whenever certain data was manually updated that could instead be electronically updated making use of the 'eGK'. Better medical treatment would further augment these savings effects. The results emphasized the benefits of the technology to payors and providers alike.

In 2007, the 'eGK' technology was tested amongst 10,000 patients in six designated areas in Germany to get representative feedback from doctors across the country. At the same time, the regions were chosen for their general political support of the new technology. However, results were mixed in terms of the technological success as well as user acceptance. This was partially due to cards not being comprehensively rolled out as well as due to technical issues, such as problems with the interoperability of components produced by different suppliers. A heavy reliance on a strong and supportive lobby within the test regions, which could mediate between the different stakeholders involved, also proved an obstacle.

In 2009, in a position paper, the umbrella organization of the payors, the GKV-SV, called for the disentanglement of the technological complexity. The idea was to reduce the dependency of the various technical components on one another, leverage the immediate economic benefits as well as increase the planning reliability for the various stakeholders involved in the rollout process. This was welcomed by the private industry, i.e. the medical technology providers. Indeed, the latter were, on the one hand, hoping to profitably supply new technologies as part of the 'eGK' solution, but, on the other hand, had previously been developing 'eGK'-related technologies that were becoming obsolete as requirements changed over time. One example of this are the so-called dual 'eGK' card reading terminals, which could also be used as payment devices in connection with credit and debit cards. As of 2004 patients were required by law to pay a quarterly charge for registration with their doctor. However, this charge was suspended in late 2012 therefore also defying the purpose of a dual card reading terminal.

Finally, in late 2010, the GKV-SV ordered yet another re-evaluation of the costs and benefits of the projects with the aim of quickly introducing a technologically simplified solution. Again, the aim was to speed up the nationwide rollout process while quickly offering the first benefits to payors, providers and patients alike. Furthermore, by then a number of risks had evolved which urgently needed to be addressed, especially from the standpoint of the payor organizations: Firstly, the rollout process of the 'eGK' had turned into a loss-making project over the years. The qualitative as well as the economic benefits of the technology, as described in earlier position papers, were becoming harder and harder to realize. Secondly, the prolonged rollout process had led to an establishment of isolated stakeholder-specific solutions. Thereby, doctors would employ competing alternative technologies to the 'eGK', such as the online payment tool KV-SafeNet or a card-based solution used by dentists, "Zahnärzte Online Deutschland", in order to electronically share patient data within their local networks. The risk of the 'eGK' technology becoming obsolete was therefore increasing. Thirdly, while the 'eGK' itself was to replace the KVK as of October 2011, the patient's master data would only be saved on the protected area of the 'eGK' once the 'eGK' technology as a whole was fully rolled out and actually connected online. Otherwise, data would be stored on an unprotected area of the microchip of the card as already the case with the KVK. Indeed, this meant that the BSI and BfDI, which had previously criticized the KVK as unsafe, could be inclined to stop the overall project for non-compliance with the required data safety and data security standards.

## 2.6.2   The Implementation Process of the 'eGK' Technology as of Today and as Currently Envisioned for the Future

As a reaction to the complications in the rollout process and the substantially prolonged implementation, the government decided to force the payor organizations to exchange the old KVK with the new 'eGK', not at least as a symbolic gesture that the implementation of the 'eGK' technology was moving ahead. The exchange of the cards was to be carried out by 31st January 2013. The insurant were hence asked to send in a mug shot to be printed onto the new cards. Those statutory health insurance companies that would not comply were to be economically penalized. Despite smaller difficulties, because some of the insurant sent fake photos of themselves, the 'eGK' itself has been handed out to basically all citizens who are statutorily ensured. Current estimates suggest that only around 2 million insurant still use the KVK which approximates to 3 % of the statutorily insured (Spiegel Online 2014). Although doctors are still entitled to accept the KVK until 01st October 2014, the 'eGK' has officially replaced the KVK as the main proof of a legible insurance status between patient and doctor as of 01st January 2014.

Prior to the actual 'eGK' being handed out, doctors had already been encouraged to purchase a card reading terminal in 2011. During the period of April–September

2011 these were also fully subsidized by the payor organizations. Doctors were therefore reimbursed for buying from one of a number of technology providers that produce these terminals according to the technical specifications defined by the 'gematik'.

Despite these important stepping-stones, the 'eGK' technology is far from delivering on its supposed potential as of January 2014. Indeed, none of the doctors are actually connected online via the 'eGK' technology as described in Sect. 2.5. While patients can now show their 'eGK', the doctors' practices cannot make any use of it as they have not been provided with the rest of the technology required.

At the time of writing, two consortia commissioned by the 'gematik' in December 2013 are working on the implementation of a new round of field tests in two designated areas, one in the counties of Schleswig-Holstein, North Rhine-Westphalia and Rhineland-Palatinate (test region Northwest), the other in Saxony and Bavaria (test region Southeast). The tendering process of the technology used in the tests incorporated three lots: two lots for the decentralized components in one of each of the test regions, i.e. all components within the doctors' medical practices necessary for the execution of the testing, and a third lot for the centralized parts of the 'eGK' technology equally applicable to both test regions, i.e. the backbone. During the field tests at least 500 doctors, dentists, psychotherapists as well as five hospitals will be connected online using the 'eGK' technology. The tests focus on assessing the functionality of mainly three features: the updating of the patients' master data, the QES (definition below) as well as the safe online connection of dental practices. The test procedure is divided into three phases: the development, the installation and the service of an actionable version of the 'eGK' technology. The tests are set to start in 2014 and will immediately be followed by the countrywide rollout.

An important milestone during this rollout process is the introduction of the so-called qualified electronic signature (Qualifizierte Elektronische Signatur—'QES'). The QES is the technical precondition for many further medical features the 'eGK' shall encompass in the future. Just as the different technological parts within the 'eGK' technology, i.e. the card reading terminal and Connector, are certified to allow for the specific and safe electronic transmission of data among them, each doctor will be issued a qualified electronic signature. This will allow them to authorize themselves and safely communicate with one another. As such, this technical function constitutes the basis for introducing features such as the electronic doctor letter, as described above.

### 2.6.3 Resistance to the 'eGK' Technology Implementation Process

Finally, at this point it is important to notice that throughout the implementation process, German doctors have repeatedly voiced their concerns in reaction to further advancements to roll out the 'eGK' technology, for example at the Congresses for Physicians (Ärztetag) in 2007, 2008, 2009, 2010, 2012 and 2013. Among other reasons, concerns were voiced that the 'eGK' technology would not be able to provide a modern, safe and user-friendly platform for the exchange of medical data.

## 2.7 Summary of the Contextual Background

Overall, the lengthy, costly as well as technically and logistically complicated implementation process of the 'eGK' technology, which has required the attention of many key stakeholders in the German healthcare sector since 2003, demonstrates the complexity of this national eHealth project. It also highlights, from a practical standpoint, some of the key characteristics or issues of such an implementation program:

- Involvement of many stakeholders—Given that healthcare is a sector that is both of great national interest as well as highly structured and regulated, it is not surprising that a lot of stakeholders are directly involved in the implementation of a national eHealth program such as the 'eGK' project. This alone is sufficient to cause delays, as coordination amongst them can be time-consuming.
- Different goals of these stakeholders—In addition to the previous point, individual parties will aim to maximize their personal utility from any project. This is particularly the case when there are numerous parties engaged in a project with potentially very high costs, both monetary as well as in terms of time and labor. Often this can also be at the expense of the utility of other parties and can further be nurtured by discrepancies surrounding the power of the stakeholders. For example, in the case of the 'eGK' implementation, the payors bear the financial costs of the project, while the providers bear the cost of having to adapt to the new system at a potential loss of their acquired working practices. Hence, their goals during the technology implementation process might differ considerably.
- Technological and logistical complexity—Generally, implementing new technology can be very complex. For example new technological standards have to be developed, subsequently local hard- and software has to be adapted and users have to be trained. In the case of a mega project, such as the implementation of the 'eGK' technology, which is to connect thousands of healthcare providers across the country with standardized eHealth technology, the complexity takes on even greater proportions.
- Data privacy and data security concerns—As medical data is some of the most sensitive out there, general concerns for data privacy and data security are naturally very high amongst patients and doctors alike. An eHealth technology required to handle such data has to be of the highest security standards. In the case of the 'eGK' technology this is clearly reflected by the involvement of

several government bodies cooperating with the 'gematik' and the medical technology industry to develop customized technology according to tailored functional and technical requirements.

With the practical background of the case established, this thesis goes on to review the relevant academic literature on national eHealth programs to get an overview on how other academics have approached the introduction of eHealth technologies from a theoretical standpoint.

# Chapter 3
# Theoretical Foundations

## 3.1 Literature on 'User Resistance Theory'

Over the years, information systems research has focused heavily on theoretical contributions around technology acceptance, adoption or diffusion. 345 articles have been published on these theories over the past 20 years which can be found within the Science Citation Index or within the Social Science Citation Index (Dwivedi et al. 2011; Williams et al. 2009). A variety of models, i.e. the Theory of Reasoned Action (TRA), the Technology Acceptance Model (TAM), the Theory of Planned Behavior (TPB), the Innovation Diffusion Theory (IDT) and the Unified Theory of Acceptance and Use of Technology (UTAUT) as well as a combination of them have been employed by researchers to explain these phenomena (Ajzen 1985; Fishbein and Ajzen 1975; Rogers 1962; Venkatesh and Davis 2000; Venkatesh 2000; Venkatesh et al. 2003). Nonetheless, the more recently advanced theory of user resistance and its implications for theory and practice should not be ignored.

User resistance, as previously defined in Sect. 1.1.1 of this thesis, has often been considered as the opposite of acceptance (Venkatesh and Davis 2000; Venkatesh et al. 2003). More recently, however, user resistance has also been identified as a differentiated factor for successful information system implementation as researchers have started building on findings dating back as early as the 1980s (Markus 1983). Indeed, various studies discuss that acceptance and resistance should not be treated as plain opposites given that the inhibitors to system usage, i.e. perceptions about a system's attributes, often differ from positive beliefs about the same system. The absence of beliefs therefore does not necessarily encourage system usage (Cenfetelli 2004). Van Offenbeek et al. (2013, p. 435) clearly differentiate between acceptance and resistance and conceptualize "resistance as a separate reaction involving different behaviors and underlying mechanisms". Finally, Lapointe and Beaudry (2014, p. 4619) argue that "acceptance and resistance are mindsets comprising three dimensions: emotions, cognition, and attitudes, and that the related behaviors are manifestations of these mindset.

© Springer International Publishing Switzerland 2015
P. Klöcker, *Resistance Behavior to National eHealth Implementation Programs*,
Progress in IS, DOI 10.1007/978-3-319-17828-8_3

Conducting a systematic literature review provided a basis for singling out the theoretical contributions on user resistance within the information systems literature (Okoli and Schabram 2010; Webster and Watson 2002). Using a keyword search nine relevant articles from the most influential IS journals were identified to which another five could be added after a round of cross-referencing. These 14 theoretical contributions about user resistance theory, as shown in Table 3.1, therefore also include those, which Lapointe and Rivard (2005, p. 462) have previously classified as the papers which have "opened the black box and proposed theoretical explanations of how and why resistance occurs". They also incorporate the research contributions discussed by Dwivedi et al. (2011) in their comprehensive discussion on user resistance theory.

Table 3.1 gives an overview of the different theoretical contributions on user resistance and explains the approaches the authors have taken in developing the theory.

As indicated, the authors in Table 3.1 explain resistance pre, during and post implementation of a new information system. For example, Kim and Kankanhalli (2009) discuss how users-to-be can forestall implementation before the technology is actually put in place, while Meissonier and Houzé (2010) and Bhattcherjee and Hikmet (2007) respectively point towards user resistance during the implementation process or as a reaction to the installed technology.

It should also be noted that most studies in this field of research are based on qualitative data. Out of the studies listed above only Bhattcherjee and Hikmet (2007), Eckhardt et al. (2009) and Kim and Kankanhalli (2009), have developed and tested user resistance models on the basis of quantitative data.

Beyond summarizing the relevant literature, Table 3.2 shows whether studies examine the influence of independent variables on user resistance connected to either the individual system users themselves or their perceived organizational and societal environment. For example, independent variables associated with the individual user itself include: one's self-efficacy for change, one's resentment of a technology or one's prior experience with other system implementations. Independent variables related to the individual user's perceived organizational climate include colleague opinion or organizational support. Only Eckhardt et al. (2009) call attention to the importance of social influence on adoption and non-adoption of information systems. They therefore factor antecedents from individuals, their perceived organizational environment as well as arguably the perceived societal environment into their model, the latter by examining the effect of customers on user resistance.

## 3.2 Acceptance/Resistance Within eHealth

An additional systematic literature review using the proposed synonyms for eHealth, as suggested by Romanow et al. (2012), was conducted to identify the relevant literature both on user acceptance and user resistance within the field of

**Table 3.1** Theoretical contributions to user resistance within IS literature

| Author | Resistance theory | Timing of implementation | Qualitative/quantitative |
|---|---|---|---|
| Bhattcherjee and Hikmet (2007) | Integrated model of resistance and acceptance theory | Post-implementation | Quantitative |
| | Resistance due to change caused to workplace by IS rather than due to technology itself | | |
| Cenfetelli (2004) | Theory for existence, nature and effects of system attribute perceptions | N/A | N/A—Theoretical contribution |
| | Discouraging the use of IS due to negative perceptions which are independent from enabling beliefs and therefore have different antecedents | | |
| Eckhardt et al. (2009) | Employment of UTAUT model | Post-implementation | Quantitative |
| | Measure of impact of various social influences on adopters and non-adopters | | |
| Ferneley and Sobreperez (2006) | Compliance/resistance/workaround model | Post-implementation | Qualitative |
| | Resistance in two phases: first internal cognitive decision to resist and secondly resultant workarounds | | |
| Joshi (1991) | Equity implementation model (EIM) | Post-implementation | Qualitative |
| | Resistance as users evaluate net gain (changes in input and outcomes) compared to that of their peers | | |
| Kim and Kankanhalli (2009) | Status quo bias model | Pre-implementation | Quantitative |
| | Resistance as a behavioral measure influenced by individual and organizational factors such as self-efficacy for change or colleague opinion | | |
| Klaus and Blanton (2010) | Resistance through the lens of users' psychological contracts with IS | Post-implementation | Qualitative |
| | Resistance due to four factors: individual, system, organizational and process-related issues | | |
| Lapointe and Rivard (2005) | Multi-level resistance model | Post-implementation | Qualitative |
| | Resistance as a result of initial condition being influenced by new object at individual and group level | | |
| Lapointe and Rivard (2012) | Implementer's responses to user resistance | Post-implementation | Qualitative |
| | Classification of user responses in four categories: inaction, acknowledgement, rectification and dissuasion; measurement of their effect on intensity of resistance | | |
| Marakas and Hornik (1996) | Passive resistance misuse model | Post-implementation | Qualitative |
| | Resistance as passive-aggressive response to stresses associated with new system | | |
| Markus (1983) | Resistance due to interaction between system implemented and context of use | Post-implementation | Qualitative |

(continued)

**Table 3.1** (continued)

| Author | Resistance theory | Timing of implementation | Qualitative/ quantitative |
|---|---|---|---|
| Martinko et al. (1996) | Attribution theory/learned helplessness models | Pre- and post-implementation | N/A— Theoretical contribution |
|  | Resistance due to internal and external variables combined with individuals' prior experience with new IT |  |  |
| Meissonier and Houzé (2010) | IT Conflict-Resistance Theory (IT-CRT) model | Pre- and during implementation | Qualitative |
|  | Resistance to be considered as process embedded into IT choice and IS design |  |  |
| van Offenbeek et al. (2013) | Integrated model of resistance and acceptance theory | Pre-, during and post-implementation | Qualitative |
|  | Voluntariness a decisive driver of whether technology is accepted or resisted |  |  |

eHealth. The search was confined to studies from the past five years which address the introduction of state of the art eHealth technology. Eight relevant papers published within the most influential IS journals were isolated. These papers do not necessarily employ strict acceptance or resistance theory in the form of models of acceptance and resistance theory, such as the 'United Theory of Acceptance and Use of Technology' (Venkatesh et al. 2003) or the 'Status Quo Bias Model' (Kim and Kankanhalli 2009) respectively, but more generally describe behavioral signs of acceptance and resistance amongst users of eHealth technologies. Table 3.3 summarizes theses papers.

As was already the case for the general IS research contributions on user resistance theory, acceptance or resistance theory within the field of eHealth is mostly analyzed with the use of qualitative data. However, two of the studies test for user acceptance in a quantitative model and also derive conclusions about user resistance behavior. Heart et al. (2011) point to physicians' non-compliance with drug prescription systems whenever they do not believe in the system's ability to generate adequate recommendations or when they feel that the system undermines their professional efficacy. Venkatesh et al. (2011, p. 541) refer "to doctors' acculturation and commitment to traditional medical practices that do not provide a key role for computer-based systems".

While only these two authors test tangible variables for user behavior towards eHealth technology, their findings are strongly supported by some of the other qualitative studies. Indeed, the importance of gaining doctors' support in order to successfully introduce eHealth technology is a notion repeatedly voiced. Doctors should not only be considered as key users of the technology, but also as key stakeholders which can uphold the successful implementation of new eHealth

**Table 3.2**  Classification of user resistance literature

| Study | Characteristics | Independent variables connected to user's... | | |
|---|---|---|---|---|
| | | ...personal characteristics | ...perceived organizational environment | ...perceived societal environment |
| Bhattcherjee and Hikmet (2007) | eHealth systems | X | | |
| Cenfetelli (2004) | N/A | N/A—Theoretical contribution | | |
| Eckhardt et al. (2009) | CV databases | X | X | X |
| Ferneley and Sobreperez (2006) | 1. Automated order system 2. Public sector reporting system | X | X | |
| Joshi (1991) | 1. Clinical laboratory system 2. Banking system | X | X | |
| Kim and Kankanhalli (2009) | Enterprise portal and knowledge management system | X | X | |
| Klaus and Blanton (2010) | Various enterprise systems | X | X | |
| Lapointe and Rivard (2005) | eHealth systems | X | X | |
| Lapointe and Rivard (2012) | Various enterprise systems | N/A | | |
| Marakas and Hornik (1996) | Unspecified enterprise system | X | X | |
| Markus (1983) | Financial information system | X | X | |
| Martinko et al. (1996) | Unspecified enterprise system | X | X | |
| Meissonier and Houzé (2010) | Enterprise resource planning system | X | X | |
| van Offenbeek et al. (2013) | eHealth system | X | X | |

technologies (Currie 2012). Similarly, Rivard et al. (2011) point to physicians' medical dominance as well as their status and autonomy which can be undermined by eHealth technology in turn leading to user resistance.

Another key finding observed through the literature review is the limited focus on the impact of societal forces on user behavior. Only Azad and King (2012, p. 370) describe the influence which "top-down extra-organizational institutionalized environments (policies and standards...)" can have on medical practitioners' workaround practices. This seems surprising given that Currie's (2012) recent study highlights the importance which perceived isomorphic forces can play in shaping

**Table 3.3** Sample of representative studies in eHealth

| Paper | eHealth technology examined | Qualitative/ quantitative | Discussion of user resistance | Focus on perceived external forces |
|---|---|---|---|---|
| Azad and King (2008) | Medication dispensing system | Qualitative | x | N/A |
| Azad and King (2012) | Medication dispensing system | Qualitative | x | Institutional theory |
| Heart et al. (2011) | Drug Prescription Notification system | Quantitative | x | N/A |
| Rivard and Lapointe (2012) | Case survey—therefore various eHealth technologies | Qualitative | x | |
| Rivard et al. (2011) | Electronic patient care | Qualitative | x | |
| Van Offenbeek et al. (2013) | Home telecare | Qualitative | XX | |
| Romanow et al. (2012) | N/A—literature review | | x | |
| Venkatesh et al. (2011) | Electronic patient care | Quantitative | x | |

*x* descriptive mention of user resistance
*XX* theoretical contribution to user resistance

the introduction of eHealth technology, a notion heavily supported in other relevant literature on eHealth (Currie and Guah 2007; Jensen et al. 2009; Mekonnen and Sahay 2008; Miscione 2007; Noir and Walsham 2007; Sahay et al. 2009).

Finally, in treating the phenomenon of user resistance, the majority of the papers are descriptive in nature. Only van Offenbeek et al. (2013) offer a theoretical discussion of user resistance as they explore the patient's perspective on the introduction of home telecare. The authors name the fear of losing contact to human medical staff, the lack of widespread knowledge on the conditions of the telecare system or financial factors as critical reasons for user resistance. The study, furthermore, shows how doctors support the use of eHealth technology in medical settings without, however, feeling the obligation to use it themselves, a phenomenon also described elsewhere (Melas et al. 2013). Amongst the more descriptive user resistance papers, Azad and King (2008) explain computer workarounds as a result of interpretive flexibility applied to rules in a professionally oriented organizational environment. Melas et al. (2013, p. 12) find that most of the medical staff is skeptical about new eHealth technology. Although physicians might actually be "'evolutionary' in their thinking, they are driven by a sense of practicality and need to be convinced of the benefits of technology".

All in all, despite Romanow et al.'s (2012) recent assertion that the phenomenon of user resistance is a key theme to the field of eHealth, a further examination of the literature shows that discussions around user resistance are often rather vague and

**Table 3.4** Studies on institutional forces within eHealth

| Author | Program/country studied | Reasons for success/failure | Theory discussed | Quantitative/ qualitative |
|--------|-------------------------|-----------------------------|------------------|---------------------------|
| Currie and Guah (2007) | NPfIT—U.K. | Conflicting institutional logics, i.e. conflicting forces in the interpretation, legitimation and mobilization of the program | Institutional theory | Qualitative |
| Currie (2012) | NPfIT—U.K. | Need to understand coercive, mimetic and normative pressures in order to fully understand outcomes of national IT programs | Institutional theory | Qualitative |
| Jensen et al. (2009) | Denmark | Challenge to doctors' authority | Institutional theory and sense-making theory | Qualitative |
|  |  | Ambiguity amongst doctors |  |  |
| Mekonnen and Sahay (2008) | Ethiopia | Absence of standards amongst regions makes scaling impossible | Institutional theory | Qualitative |
|  |  | Presence of institutional-organizational relationship facilitates scaling |  |  |
| Miscione (2007) | Peru | Telemedicine-based health development is weakly accountable to local social contexts and their diversity | New institutionalism | Qualitative |
| Noir and Walsham (2007) | India | Decoupling takes place, i.e. organizational goals are constructed to be ambiguous, harmonization and integration are resisted | New institutionalism | Qualitative |
| Sahay et al. (2009) | India | Uneven distribution of power between large institutional organizations and small companies | Integration theory | Qualitative |
|  |  | Therefore need for configurability of product flexibility and timing |  |  |

more of a by-product of findings from studies with a much broader focus. Indeed, the studies here observed leave room for interpretation as well as for deriving a discrete set of variables which can be deductively or empirically tested to explain user resistance amongst physicians.

## 3.3 Isomorphic Forces Within eHealth

As already hinted at above, most relevant studies on eHealth lay their focus on implementation programs at an organizational level, i.e. a single hospital. This is confirmed by a third systematic literature review building on Romanow et al.'s (2012) literature review on the topic of eHealth within IS, whereby their exact search criteria were used to update their study with another 14 papers published in one of the most influential journals of the IS field.

A subsequent screening of all 232 papers for those that examine large-scale eHealth implementation programs beyond just a limited number of organizations or hospitals shows, that only 33 papers truly examine eHealth implementation on a national scale. By looking at countrywide eHealth programs, for example in the U.K., the U.S., Denmark and several emerging countries, these studies offer an extensive yet not always consistent list of explanations for why such large-scale programs can fail: high initial expectations (Sauer and Willcocks 2007), long-term immobility of large stakeholders (Aanestad and Jensen 2011), the failure to standardize information infrastructures (Braa et al. 2007) or the failure to understand the wider socio-political and inter-organizational environment (Currie 2012) to name some.

One common theme introduced in multiple papers, however, is that of 'societal' or 'isomorphic' or 'institutional' forces (please also refer back to the definition in the introductory section of this thesis). According to the literature these can be a key impact factor for large-scale eHealth implementation programs. As Davidson and Chismar (2007) explain, institutional and technological changes are often closely related. From the 33 papers, seven papers could be identified that examine the effects of institutional forces (summarized in Table 3.4). Noticeably, all 33 papers on national eHealth programs are case studies based on qualitative data, suggesting that the influence of institutional factors has not been examined using quantitative data in the context of national eHealth programs.

# Chapter 4
# Phase I—Pilot Study

## 4.1 Model Development

From the literature review above it can be concluded that the field of eHealth is yet missing a quantitative empirical study that verifies the specific antecedents leading to user resistance of eHealth technologies. Given the complexity of many national eHealth implementation programs, as in the case of the German 'eGK' technology, the following section describes a pilot study conducted to verify resistance-related antecedents previously identified in other information systems studies in the context of eHealth. This section therefore runs through the analysis of an existing resistance model in order to examine the applicability of current user resistance theory to the context of the German 'eGK' technology. For this purpose, the 'Status Quo Bias Model' developed by Kim and Kankanhalli (2009) is used and the effects of the antecedents therein defined are measured. Overall, this section aims at answering the first of the two research questions initially posited:

> *Research Question 1: Is the case of the introduction of the 'eGK' technology one of user resistance theory and do previously developed antecedents appropriately explain user resistance in the context of the 'eGK' technology?*

The 'Status Quo Bias Model' builds on the notion that people have a "preference for maintaining their current status or situation" (Kim and Kankanhalli 2009, p. 569). According to Samuelson and Zeckhauser (1988) this is true for three reasons: rational decision-making, cognitive misperceptions or psychological commitment. An individual therefore rationally selects the alternative with the highest expected utility (rational decision making), is likely to weigh potential losses incurred from a switch higher than potential gains (cognitive misperception) and is psychologically influenced by sunk costs in her decision making (psychological commitment). Together this leads a user to maintain the status quo over adopting a new technology.

© Springer International Publishing Switzerland 2015
P. Klöcker, *Resistance Behavior to National eHealth Implementation Programs*,
Progress in IS, DOI 10.1007/978-3-319-17828-8_4

Furthermore, Bhattacherjee and Hikmet (2007) discuss that "social systems share with biological systems the characteristic of "homeostasis", or the tendency to maintain status quo by resisting change and reverting back to the original state", further supporting the notion of status quo bias.

The 'Status Quo Bias Model' is particularly well suited for conducting this pilot study because it builds on well-established constructs and items applicable to IS implementation in varying contexts. It is moreover especially fitting to the context of eHealth. Within this context doctors are said to take great pride in their traditional ways of working and to be strongly inclined to retain the status quo: "Because IT (such as clinical decision support systems) may, to certain degree, codify expert knowledge possessed by physicians and the problem-solving process previously known only to physicians, physicians may perceive it as threatening to their professional autonomy" (Walter and Lopez 2008, p. 208).

## 4.2  Hypotheses of the 'Status Quo Bias Model'

As discussed by Kahneman and Tversky (1979) and Kim and Kankanhalli (2009, p. 571), *perceived value* is conceptualized as the "perceived net benefits relative to the costs of a new information system-related change". The concept of perceived value therefore suggests that users will always evaluate the benefits of switching to the new technology against their relative costs. This implies that, if the perceived value of the new technology is low, users are more likely to resist it given that they tend to maximize their personal value in their decision making process. It is proposed:

*H1: Perceived value has a negative effect on user resistance.*

*Switching costs* are conceptualized as the "perceived disutility a user would incur in switching from the status quo to the new IS" (Kim and Kankanhalli 2009, p. 572). As per status quo bias theory switching costs include the transition costs, the uncertainty costs, and the sunk costs associated with switching to the new technology (Samuelson and Zeckhauser 1988). Switching costs are likely to have a direct effect on user resistance. Indeed, the three types of costs bias a user towards retaining the status quo through transient costs, the feeling of incompetence and lastly the resistance to forgo past investments. Thus:

*H2: Switching costs have a positive effect on user resistance.*

Switching costs will also affect user resistance indirectly through perceived value. Higher switching costs can therefore be expected to decrease the net benefit of a change to the new information system, negatively affecting the perceived value of this information system (Kim and Kankanhalli 2009). Therefore:

*H3: Switching costs have a negative effect on perceived value.*

*Switching benefits* can be defined as the "perceived utility a user would enjoy in switching from the status quo to the new IS" (Kim and Kankanhalli 2009, p. 573).

Such benefits for example include enhanced personal performance or new rewards directly associated with the switch to the new technology. This will increase the value of switching:

*H4: Switching benefits have a positive effect on perceived value.*

The ease with which users can master potential challenges as well as avoid the threats associated with the switch to the new information system is represented by *self-efficacy for change*. Self-efficacy for change therefore describes an individual's confidence in his or her own ability to adapt to the new information system (Bandura 1997; Klaus and Blanton 2010; Martinko et al. 1996). In other words, a person comfortable with her own capabilities is less likely to resist the introduction of a new technology. At the same time, high self-efficacy for change means that users are less anxious or uncertain about a switch to a new system. They will also tackle the adaption and possible learning in a focused manner. High self-efficacy for change is therefore said to decrease uncertainty and transition costs (Kim and Kankanhalli 2009). Therefore:

*H5: Self-efficacy for change has a negative effect on user resistance.*
*H6: Self-efficacy for change has a negative effect on switching costs.*

*Organizational support* is the perceived facilitation provided by the organization which helps users adapt to the new information system and affords users with the necessary guidance to adapt to the changes related to the new information system (Hirschheim and Newman 1988; Kim and Kankanhalli 2009). Therefore, as the organization provides more training and other relevant resources, users might react less negatively to the newly implemented information system:

*H7: Organizational support for change has a negative effect on user resistance.*

Lewis et al. (2003) argue that management support for a technology increases the ease of use of the technology. Equally therefore organizational support for change can reduce a user's switching costs as training and other relevant resources reduce the user's perceived difficulty in adapting to the new technology:

*H8: Organizational support for change has a negative effect on switching costs.*

Kim and Kankanhalli (2009, p. 573) define *colleague opinion* as the "perception that colleagues favor the changes related to a new IS implementation". The authors suggest that colleagues influence each other in a normative fashion. As such, when a user sees colleagues with the new technology she might either perceive the need for companionship or, on the contrary, might fear being sanctioned for non-compliance (Ajzen 2002; Lewis et al. 2003):

*H9: Favorable colleague opinion has a negative effect on user resistance.*

Arguably users internalize the information obtained from their colleagues. This too will alter their perception of switching costs and benefits (Burnkrant and Cousineau 1975). A colleague's positive opinion about the new information system can therefore reduce another user's uncertainty over this new system. This can either

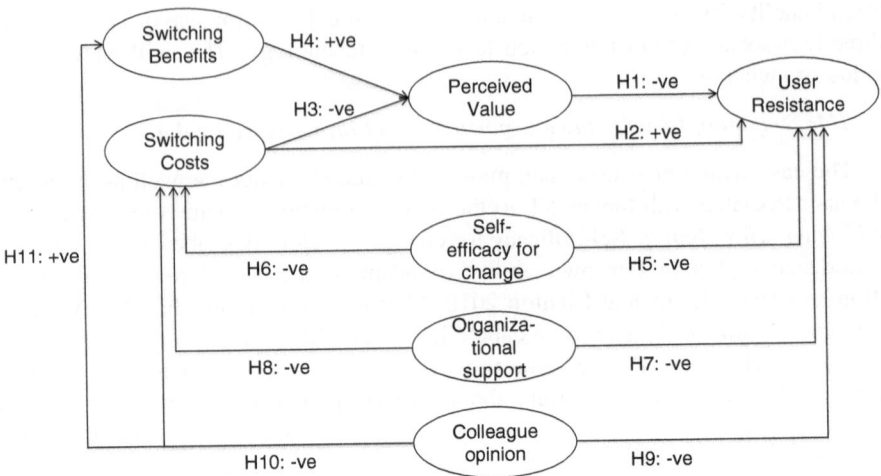

**Fig. 4.1** Model for pilot study ('Status Quo Bias Model'). *Note* Adapted from Kim and Kankanhalli (2009)

lead to a decrease in perceived switching costs or it can equally lead to an increase in perceived switching benefits. Thus:

> *H10: Favorable colleague opinion has a negative effect on switching costs.*
> *H11: Favorable colleague opinion has a positive effect on switching benefits.*

## 4.3  Research Methodology

### 4.3.1  Sample, Data Collection Procedure and Measurement of Constructs

Given that the goal of this first pilot study is to empirically test whether existing user resistance theory is applicable to the particular context of eHealth, a reasonably sized sample of quantitative data was collected, which would allow the running of the required statistical analyses. For this purpose the data was gathered through an online survey involving German doctors who will be supplied with the 'eGK' technology. All constructs are reflective measures. The items were translated into German allowing all participants to answer in their mother tongue. This ensured face and content validity of the scales (Moore and Benbasat 1991). The scales were furthermore rephrased to fit the subject of the 'eGK' technology. Given that the constructs had to be translated into German, a round of item sorting was conducted, whereby two independent groups of judges, one a group of academic researchers the other a group of subject experts, were asked to match the items with the corresponding constructs.

This ensured inter-rater reliability (Moore and Benbasat 1991). The measurement items were anchored on a seven-point Likert scale ranging from 'strongly disagree' to 'strongly agree'.

To achieve a comparability of results to Kim and Kankanhalli's (2009) original framework, the scales for user resistance, perceived value, switching benefits and costs, self-efficacy for change, organizational support and colleague opinion were based very closely on theirs, which are in turn based on validated scales.

The data was collected using an online survey distributed to 1000 doctors of different specializations across Germany. The email addresses were purchased from a specialized provider ensuring a representative sample across specialized profession (for example general practitioner, surgeon, oculist etc.), gender and region. In total, 85 doctors responded to the questionnaire, out of which 53 doctors answered the questionnaire in full. Given that respondents either started the questionnaire and aborted it immediately or answered it in full, only the responses of those who answered in full were used to test the hypotheses of the model. This phenomenon might be explained by the highly political nature of the topic around the 'eGK', whereby doctors in Germany have been known to take very extreme stances on this topic. 81 % of the 53 doctors were male. The average respondent was between 45 and 59 years old corresponding to the general average age of doctors in Germany. Overall, doctors of 16 specializations participated in the survey. Approximately 50 % of the participants were general practitioners. All doctors answered themselves, none had their receptionist answer for them.

Smart PLS Version 2.0.M3 was used to analyze the data (Ringle et al. 2005). Typically, PLS models are assessed in two stages, the first being the analysis of the "reliability and validity of the measurement model" and the second being the analysis of the structural model itself (Hulland 1999, p. 198). In order to test the validity of the model, tests using partial least squares analysis were performed, which were also recommended by other researchers (Brown and Venkatesh 2005; Chin 1998; Gefen and Straub 2005; Hulland 1999). The results are summarized in Tables 4.1 and 4.2. As such, convergent item validity is measured using three criteria: First of all, each item should load significantly on their respective constructs with the threshold of the loading often set at 0.70 or above (Gefen and Straub 2005). Two items, OGS4 and SWC1, proposed in Kim and Kankanhalli's (2009) original model did not load significantly in this pilot study and should be eliminated if the model was run again in a larger quantitative test. (For reasons of consistency these two items were kept in the model of this pilot. However, as a further check they were removed and the model was run again without them. This test did not result in any significant changes to the overall model as described in Sect. 4.3.2. Further, all other tests for validity were confirmed without the two items, too.) Secondly, Hulland (1999) suggests that the composite reliabilities should be greater than 0.70, while thirdly, the average variance extracted (AVE) for each construct should be greater than 0.50 (Bhattacherjee and Premkumar 2004). These criteria are met by the data

**Table 4.1** Item means and standard deviations, outer loadings and their statistical significance ('Status Quo Bias Model')

| Item | Mean | Standard deviation | Outer loading | T statistics ($|O/STERR|$) |
|------|------|--------------------|---------------|----------------------------|
| CGP 1 | 1.727 | 1.119 | 0.798 | 5.762 |
| CGP 2 | 1.891 | 1.216 | 0.843 | 12.051 |
| CGP 3 | 1.509 | 0.970 | 0.868 | 18.408 |
| OGS 2 | 2.818 | 1.936 | 0.938 | 4.419 |
| OGS 3 | 2.273 | 1.495 | 0.867 | 3.399 |
| OGS 4 | 1.618 | 1.355 | 0.463 | 1.276 |
| PVL 1 | 2.273 | 1.834 | 0.886 | 15.848 |
| PVL 2 | 2.400 | 1.960 | 0.952 | 41.102 |
| PVL 3 | 2.527 | 1.971 | 0.901 | 16.121 |
| RTC 1 | 4.236 | 2.544 | 0.930 | 40.031 |
| RTC 2 | 4.455 | 2.514 | 0.912 | 28.408 |
| RTC 3 | 4.582 | 2.425 | 0.834 | 14.180 |
| RTC 5 | 4.055 | 2.576 | 0.896 | 20.011 |
| SFC 1 | 3.964 | 1.972 | 0.925 | 21.314 |
| SFC 2 | 3.964 | 2.097 | 0.888 | 12.936 |
| SFC 3 | 3.818 | 2.001 | 0.883 | 20.278 |
| SWB 1 | 2.109 | 1.580 | 0.913 | 14.717 |
| SWB 2 | 2.109 | 1.592 | 0.949 | 35.632 |
| SWB 3 | 2.000 | 1.537 | 0.956 | 40.863 |
| SWB 4 | 2.109 | 1.648 | 0.939 | 31.313 |
| SWC 1 | 5.000 | 1.916 | 0.300 | 1.507 |
| SWC 2 | 4.709 | 2.112 | 0.870 | 28.066 |
| SWC 3 | 5.218 | 2.069 | 0.816 | 12.260 |
| SWC 4 | 3.782 | 2.286 | 0.781 | 9.526 |

**Table 4.2** Square root of AVEs, composite reliabilities and correlations ('Status Quo Bias Model')

| Construct | AVE | CR | 1 | 2 | 3 | 4 | 5 | 6 | 7 |
|-----------|-----|-----|-----|-----|-----|-----|-----|-----|-----|
| Colleague opinion | 0.700 | 0.875 | **0.837** | | | | | | |
| Organizational support for change | 0.615 | 0.817 | 0.322 | **0.784** | | | | | |
| Perceived value | 0.834 | 0.938 | 0.389 | 0.140 | **0.913** | | | | |
| Resistance | 0.799 | 0.941 | −0.386 | −0.230 | −0.534 | **0.894** | | | |
| Self-efficacy for change | 0.808 | 0.927 | 0.307 | 0.350 | 0.125 | −0.230 | **0.899** | | |
| Switching benefits | 0.882 | 0.968 | 0.481 | 0.168 | 0.811 | −0.582 | 0.209 | **0.939** | |
| Switching costs | 0.531 | 0.803 | −0.504 | −0.310 | −0.604 | 0.621 | −0.546 | −0.682 | **0.729** |

*Note AVE* average variance extracted; *CR* composite reliability

(please refer to Sect. 6.1 for a theoretical discussion of PLS-SEM analysis and Sect. 6.5 for a more detailed description of the meanings of these analyses in relation to the testing of the validity of the main quantitative model).

Discriminant validity is established by ensuring that the square root of AVE of a construct exceeds the correlations between this construct and the other constructs of the model (Bhattacherjee and Premkumar 2004; Fornell and Larcker 1981; Gefen and Straub 2005). As shown in Table 4.2, the square roots of all constructs are larger than the correlation of that construct with others (with the square root of the construct's AVE reported on the main diagonal; the off-diagonal cells show the correlation between that construct and the others).

### 4.3.2 Results of Hypothesis Testing

The hypotheses behind the model were tested by examining the significance of the parameter estimates. Bootstrapping with m = 1000 samples and n = 53 cases was used. The results confirmed H2, the positive effect of switching costs on user resistance ($\beta = +0.503$, $p < 0.001$) and H4, the positive effect of switching benefits on perceived value ($\beta = +0.746$, $p < 0.001$). However, they did not confirm H1 and H3, the negative effect of perceived value on user resistance and the negative effect of switching costs on perceived value respectively. The second of these findings are therefore not in line with Kim and Kankanhalli's (2009) original 'Status Quo Bias Model'.

As suggested by H6, self-efficacy for change showed a significant negative effect on switching costs ($\beta = -0.419$, $p < 0.001$). Just as in the original model, self-efficacy for change has no direct significant effect on user resistance. The effects of colleague opinion also mirror those found in the original model, with significant effects measured on switching costs ($\beta = -0.360$, $p < 0.001$) and switching benefits ($\beta = +0.481$, $p < 0.001$), but no significant direct effect on user resistance. Finally, organizational support had a direct negative effect on user resistance in Kim and Kankanhalli's (2009) model. It neither had a direct nor an indirect effect on user resistance in the model of this pilot study (Fig. 4.2).

## 4.4 Discussion of Findings

The first goal of this research was to test whether the case of the 'eGK' technology implementation is indeed one of user resistance and whether previously developed antecedents can be used to explain the resistance to such an eHealth technology. While one should be aware of the fact that this discussion is based on a relatively small data sample, all statistical measures hold and the model was able to explain a significant amount of $R^2 = 0.438$. At the same time none of the three factors,

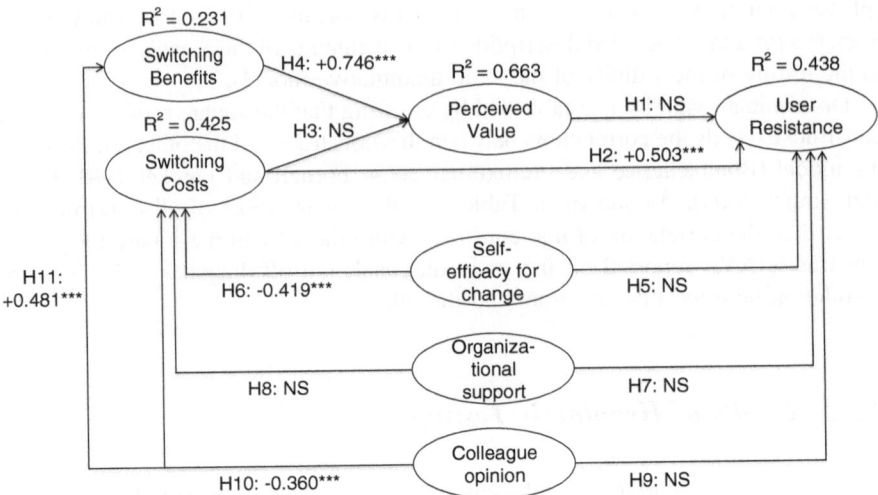

**Fig. 4.2** Results of hypothesis testing ('Status Quo Bias Model'). *Note* ***p* < 0.01; *NS* not significant at 0.1 significance level

self-efficacy for change, organizational support and colleague opinion, as suggested by Kim and Kankanhalli (2009), have a direct effect on user resistance. Indeed, only two factors indirectly load via switching costs and switching benefits respectively.

From these findings it can be concluded that user resistance is very much an appropriate dependent variable to be measured in the case of the 'eGK' technology implementation project. At the same time, however, other independent variables should be taken into consideration to better explain what drives individual physicians' resistance to this particular eHealth technology.

# Chapter 5
# Phase II—Qualitative Study

In order to gain a comprehensive understanding of the factors which more adequately explain user resistance to the 'eGK' technology, further in-depth explanatory data was collected yielding a discrete set of antecedents. The following section describes the collection and analysis of such qualitative data.

## 5.1 Data Collection Procedure

The data was collected in two phases: firstly, through the deep insight into several related implementation projects and especially the day-to-day running of a project between December 2010 and August 2011 aimed at rolling out the 'eGK'-related eHealth infrastructure to approximately 71,000 practices, 41,000 dental practices and 2000 hospitals until the end of 2012. This uniquely close involvement had the advantage of in-depth access to people, issues and data (Walsham 2006). It was therefore possible to be part of countless formal and informal meetings with members of several stakeholder groups including the 'gematik', the Federal Ministry of Health, the Federal Office of Information Security, the Federal Commissioner for Data Protection and Freedom of Information, the lead associations of payors and providers, individual health insurance companies as well as several system providers and external consultants.

In addition to these meetings, several comprehensive reports were written and countless emails were exchanged, which were used as data on this subject. Together, this rich account of the on-going activities provided an unparalleled insight into the program as it has unfolded over time. A major advantage of this method was that it allowed for taking a longitudinal perspective on the implementation process, which is especially important as "the temporal scope,...., affect[s] the apparent origin and direction of many phenomena" (Kozlowski and Klein 2000, p. 17).

Secondly, building on these insights, semi-structured interviews with 14 interview partners from the key stakeholder groups identified in the first stage of the research process and directly involved in the 'eGK' technology implementation

© Springer International Publishing Switzerland 2015
P. Klöcker, *Resistance Behavior to National eHealth Implementation Programs*,
Progress in IS, DOI 10.1007/978-3-319-17828-8_5

were conducted (please see Table A2 in the Appendix for further details on the interviews conducted). The guidelines provided by Walsham (2006) on sampling, interviewing, analysis and triangulation were followed.

The interview partners were chosen because of their expert knowledge and strong involvement as well as to represent each of the key stakeholder groups involved in the 'eGK' implementation process: 'gematik', providers, payors, the government, the medical technology industry as well as five individual doctors. Further, an external consultant who was involved at several stages of the implementation process was interviewed. The average interview lasted one hour. Patients were not interviewed, as they have not been involved in the project and have not been in touch with technology, as it is yet to be fully rolled out. Due to privacy concerns, as this is still an ongoing project, not all interview partners agreed to be recorded on voice record. Exact interview notes were, however, taken throughout all interviews. Besides, not recording interviews has also been discussed as being less critical in comparable circumstances (Goh et al. 2011; Silva and Backhouse 2003). Privacy concerns were also the reason why another three stakeholders, all from one of the stakeholder groups interviewed anyhow, did not agree to be interviewed.

## 5.2  Analysis of Data

A theme which arose out of the involvement in countless meetings with many of the stakeholders and which was also repeatedly highlighted by the interviewees was the complexity of the 'eGK' technology implementation project involving a multi-faceted network of stakeholders. In particular, the stakes of payors and providers within the 'gematik', both holding 50 %, are defined by law (§ 291a Abs. 7, SGB V). This leaves little room for maneuvering, as one party can successfully obstruct decisions by the other. At the same time, the 'gematik' is often dependent on the approval of the Federal Ministry of Health, the Federal Office for Information Security and the Federal Commissioner for Data Protection and Freedom of Information. This very same set-up has caused substantial complications in the implementation process as each party tries to enforce their point of view. One interview partner points out:

> Right from the outset, the technical and logistical planning requirements of this project were absurd.

Two interview partners therefore suggest that the founding of the 'gematik' was a means by which the government tried to improve the arrangement. At the same time they hint at the force with which the government was pushing the project as it already began stalling early on:

> Payors and providers were not able to roll out the 'eGK' technology based on a regulatory framework. This forced the government to introduce the 'gematik', which is closely regulated by the Ministry of Health.

One of them continues:

> Moreover, the government has in the past been forced to coerce solutions by decree-law because the 'gematik' would not pass them. ... In particular, the government defined the regulatory framework for the functional and technical specifications of the field tests for the 'eGK' technology [in 2007]. ... We are aware that we were forcing these decisions on users, but we had the impression that other players were happy that someone was finally taking action.

This is very relevant, as in the end the users of the 'eGK' technology will be the physicians who have to install the 'eGK' technology in their medical practices and have to incorporate it in their daily working routines. One doctor interviewed even perceived such pressure as *"fascistic"*.

Regarding the pressure that physicians perceive to be under from the payor organizations, another doctor explained:

> The payor organizations, [...] i.e. business economists, are dictating doctors what to do. Humaneness is falling by the wayside.

At the same time, doctors very much seem to value the opinion of their colleagues:

> The 'gematik' claims that the field tests in 2007 worked smoothly. In fact, my colleagues who participated in those test disagree vehemently.

Besides, the physicians interviewed repeatedly voiced their concerns about the risks associated with regards to data privacy and data security of online technologies, such as the 'eGK' technology:

> Data privacy can never be ensured. I would prefer an alternative [offline] solution, whereby the patient carries a 'patient book', which contains her medical history and which she can take back home.

Indeed, as highlighted earlier, medical data is some of the most sensitive and has to be treated delicately. Personal meetings with the Federal Office of Information Security, the Federal Commissioner for Data Protection and Freedom of Information stressed the seriousness with which this matter is being discussed.

Overall, the following statements emphasize the general resistance of doctors towards the 'eGK' technology:

> This technology is idiotic and is wasting billions of Euros…The human being is becoming less and less important. or

> My opinion of the 'eGK' is a particularly bad one. I cannot accept that we are using money out of health funds to subsidize the IT sector.

Another physician adds:

> The 'eGK' is the icing on the cake that is the squandering of billions [of Euros].

Moreover, patients and the general public have in recent months been made increasingly aware of the technology as the payor organizations were forced to provide their insurant with the new 'eGK' until the end of 2013. This has had opposing effects: While it has increased general awareness for the technology, it has also caused confusion amongst patients and doctors as the card itself without the underlying technology has no functional eHealth-related value. Furthermore, technical difficulties associated with the release process have caught on negatively amongst patients and the press. One interviewee states:

> I have had phone calls from the insurant complaining about the release procedure of the card. They threatened to go to the press with their problems.

Finally, however, one doctor admits:

> Some of my patients welcome the 'eGK' technology and will possibly prefer to go to doctors that use the technology in the future.

## 5.3  Discussion of Findings

Using the qualitative data on the case of the German 'eGK' technology two phenomena in particular seem to explain the problems associated with rolling out this eHealth technology. Firstly, the interview partners discussed the complex network of stakeholders involved in this national eHealth implementation program. Specifically, they pointed towards the stakeholders' often-assertive conduct with which they tried to enforce their very own goals in this program. Secondly, concerns over data privacy were repeatedly voiced by many of the interview partners.

When linking these phenomena to the individual doctors who will eventually be employing this technology, it is important to keep in mind that in Germany, like in many other countries, they have thus far benefitted from great liberties in their ways of working (Kohli and Kettinger 2004; Rivard et al. 2011; Romanow et al. 2012; Venkatesh et al. 2011). Doctors might therefore understand the introduction of the 'eGK' technology as an infringement by the payors, the 'gematik' and the government. According to the data both the government and the payor organizations have put direct pressure on providers and vice versa, as each party tries to shape the 'eGK' implementation project in their best interest. Currie and Guah (2007, p. 236) discuss such an entanglement as "exogenous influences on institutional environments […] exerted in the form of societal and regulatory pressures that seek to alter the material-resource environment and the value systems".

Another noteworthy stakeholder behavior observed revolves around the norms and standards which the government has recently put in place. Thus, payor organizations were forced to replace patients' KVK with the new 'eGK' in order to accelerate the overall rollout process and create increased awareness amongst doctors and patients alike. This was confirmed by some of the interviewees, as discussed in the quotes above. Depending on one's viewpoint, such measures might be perceived as the government either creating important standards or coercively enforcing project development. However, given that the technology as a whole has not been installed in medical practices and the card itself therefore has no eHealth related use, this move has also caused substantial confusion.

Finally, over the years the medical technology industry has repeatedly voiced their interest in designing and supplying the technology around the 'eGK', not at least due to the prospect of profitable business opportunities. With the aim of gaining a first mover advantage some providers have already developed working technological solutions. This, again, can be understood as a sign that sector-wide standards are being created. Davidson and Chismar (2007) discuss such change as the close relationship between institutional and technological changes.

Klöcker (2014) sums up the stakeholder interaction in the case of the 'eGK' technology implementation project and integrates the key stakeholders involved in this specific project into a single framework (see Fig. 5.1). In particular, it can be observed that these stakeholders act on three levels. From an individual doctor's perspective, these are: the perceived societal level including players such as the government or the umbrella organizations of both payors and providers, the

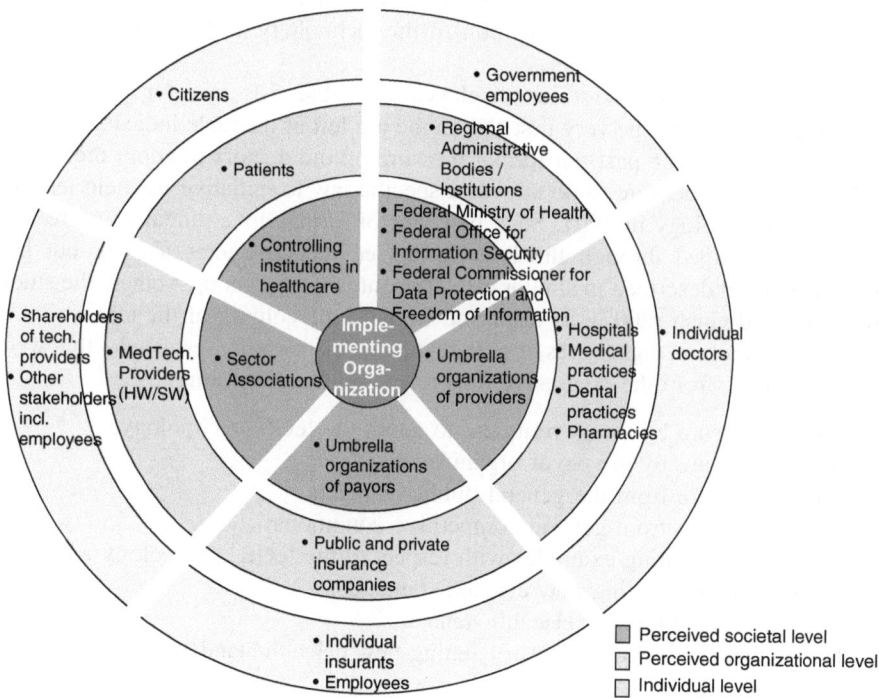

**Fig. 5.1**  Stakeholder model. *Note* adapted from Klöcker (2014)

perceived organizational level and the individual level. The author therefore points out that conflicts amongst stakeholders can arise as these put intra-level pressure, i.e. between the government and umbrella organizations, as well as inter-level pressure, i.e. between the government and individual doctors, on one another. Indeed, as discussed in Sect. 3.3, the screening of Romanow et al.'s literature review revealed another seven papers which also examine the effects of similar societal forces on national eHealth implementation projects and confirm their importance in shaping their success (Currie 2012; Currie and Guah 2007; Jensen et al. 2009; Mekonnen and Sahay 2008; Miscione 2007; Noir and Walsham 2007; Sahay et al. 2009).

The goal of the qualitative study was to derive a set of tangible variables which influence doctors' resistance behavior towards the 'eGK' technology. The findings from the qualitative data as well as the key themes extracted from the relevant literature discussed above provide such a set of tangible variables which can be tested in a quantitative model. The variables are therefore generated to mirror the behavior of the key stakeholders within the 'eGK' technology implementation project as each of them tries to enforce their point of view. The quantitative model designed on this basis focuses on the actions these stakeholders take towards physicians resting on the condition that they will effectively be the ones using the 'eGK' technology on a daily basis. Furthermore, it is this stakeholder group which has largely resisted the implementation of the technology so far. Table 5.1 summarizes the observed behaviors.

The stakeholder behavior, as displayed in Table 5.1, can for example be explained as follows: The very first 'X' on the top left of the table indicates that the government has in the past put formal pressure on the doctors to adopt the 'eGK' technology. One measure to do so was a specific law to initiative the field tests of the 'eGK' technology in 2007. Such behavior of formal government pressure was not only confirmed through the interviews (see related quotes above), but has previously been described in similar eHealth contexts too, amongst others the study by Currie and Guah (2007), as displayed in the same column of the table.

Overall therefore, eight types of societal behaviors towards German doctors were observed either from the qualitative data or the relevant literature:

1. Formal pressure by the government to adopt the 'eGK' technology,
2. Formal pressure by the payor organizations,
3. Formal pressure from the general public or media,
4. Formal pressure from general competitive conditions,
5. Other doctors setting examples with respect to the 'eGK' technology adoption,
6. The government setting new eHealth standards,
7. Patients demanding new eHealth standards,
8. The medical technology industry setting new eHealth standards.

The effect of these behaviors on physicians' user resistance to the 'eGK' technology is to be tested in a quantitative model.

**Table 5.1** Physicians' perceived environment—actions by stakeholder

| Source | Stakeholder behavior towards physicians | Stakeholders | | | | | | |
|---|---|---|---|---|---|---|---|---|
| | | Government | Payor organizations | The general public/media | Other doctors | Patients | Med-tech industry | Competitive conditions |
| **Qualitative data** | Formal pressure | X | X | | | | | X |
| | Following others' examples | | | | X | | | |
| | Setting new standards | | | | | X | X | |
| **Relevant literature on eHealth (examples)** | Formal pressure | Currie and Guah (2007) | | Currie (2012) | Jensen et al. (2009) | | | |
| | Following others' examples | | | | | | | |
| | Setting new standards | Mekonnen and Sahay (2008) | | | | (Currie 2012) | Sahay et al. (2009) | |

Besides, and as already pointed out in the data analysis above, the factor of data privacy concerns was repeatedly voiced by interview partners as a key aspect to be addressed during the implementation of the 'eGK' technology. This factor is added to the quantitative model, too. The doctors interviewed as part of the qualitative data expressed related concerns about the security of their patient data which will in the future be transmitted online. Given the sensitive nature of healthcare data, the literature within the field of eHealth has also pointed to the significance of data privacy (Bansal et al. 2010; Earp and Payton 2006; Rindfleisch 1997; Xu et al. 2011).

# Chapter 6
# Phase III—Quantitative Study

## 6.1 Methodology

Before this thesis goes on to explain the concrete hypotheses derived from the qualitative data and the relevant literature as discussed above, the following section briefly describes the methodology of Structural Equation Modeling (SEM). SEM was already used to analyze the data in the Pilot Study of Phase I. It is furthermore used to draw up the path model derived from the findings of the qualitative data analyzed in Phase II, which is subsequently tested with the large quantitative data set in Phase III of this research. In particular, the section below discusses the choice of the methodology employed and the measurement mode in the form of reflective as opposed to formative constructs. The choice of model is accounted for in detail before this thesis proceeds to explain the actual data collection procedure and measurements of the quantitative model from Sect. 6.2 onwards.

### 6.1.1 Structural Equation Modeling

Today structural equation modeling is regarded as a standard method used to evaluate quantitative data in the field of information systems research. Moreover it is also a standard in other areas of research such as Marketing (Babin et al. 2008; Hulland 1999). SEM belongs to the category of multivariate analyses and as such is a statistical tool to simultaneously analyze multiple variables. These typically relate to individuals, companies, situations etc. and are normally obtained from surveys or other forms of observation which provide adequate primary or secondary data (Hair et al. 2013).

Given this set-up, SEM offers potential advantages over linear regression models, which are often described as first-generation techniques. As part of the second-generation techniques, which include confirmatory factor analyses for example, SEM

© Springer International Publishing Switzerland 2015
P. Klöcker, *Resistance Behavior to National eHealth Implementation Programs*,
Progress in IS, DOI 10.1007/978-3-319-17828-8_6

enables researchers to include latent variables into their model. These are indirectly measured by indicator variables. Furthermore, it allows for better observation of measurement error within the measured variables (Chin 1998; Hair et al. 2013).

A latent variable, also referred to as a theoretical *construct*, cannot be measured directly through the assignment of numbers unlike concrete variables, i.e. gender could be divided into 0 for male and 1 for female. A latent variable is more complex, i.e. a belief, an intention or the trust in something. It is therefore measured indirectly through a set of proxies, representing the various aspects of the variable and together forming the larger abstract concept. One of these proxies is also referred to as a *manifest variable* or an *item*. The items will be measured using *coding* which facilitates the process. In a questionnaire, for example, the respondent will be offered a statement relating to the measurement of her belief or intention and can then choose along a so-called Likert-scale (common in SEM context) from 1 = *strongly disagree* to 7 = *strongly agree* to state her response. It is important to ensure symmetry of Likert items over a middle category so as to keep equidistance (Hair et al. 2013).

Measuring latent variables through items can lead to measurement errors as there is a distinction between the measures and the measured variables. This measurement error should be accounted for using appropriate techniques that help reduce the effect (Rigdon 1994).

The relationship between variables as measured by SEM is often displayed in path models (Hair et al. 2011a, b). A theoretical example of such a path model is shown in Fig. 6.1 (while Fig. 6.3 in Sect. 6.3 displays the path model including the

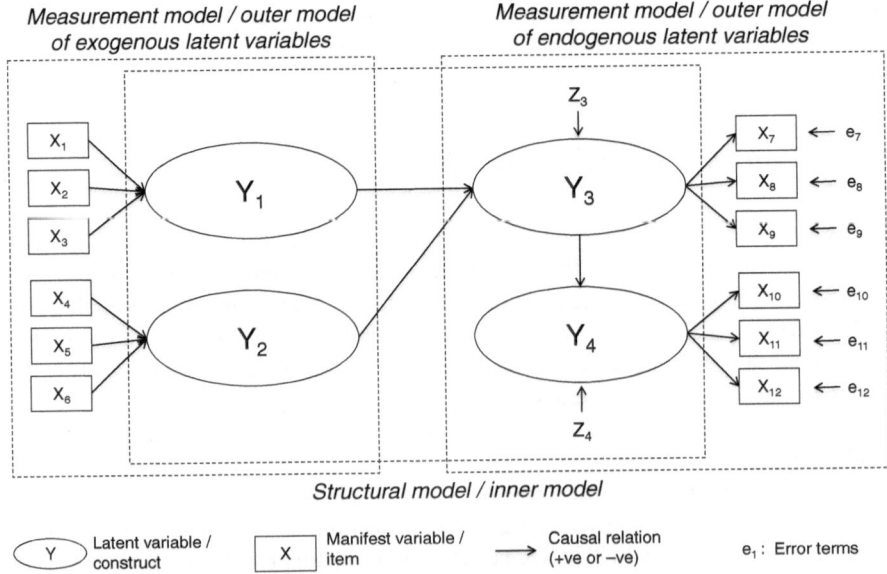

**Fig. 6.1** Theoretical path model. *Note* Adapted from Hair et al. (2013)

paths and hypotheses within the quantitative research model of this study on the 'eGK'). The path model therefore exhibits the relationship between the latent variables (constructs = $Y_{1-4}$) and manifest variables (items = $X_{1-10}$) which contain the raw data. It also shows the relationship between individual constructs. The single-headed arrows represent a predictive relationship.

The inner or structural model represents the constructs and their relationships only. The measure of the construct through the items is described at the outer or measurement level (Bollen 1989; Hair et al. 2013). The constructs within the inner model are divided into endogenous and exogenous variables. An endogenous variable is so categorized if it is influenced by other constructs according to the predictive relationship of the structural model. The exogenous variables, however, are solely determined by their respective items, i.e. the exogenous variable $Y_2$ is therefore only explained by its respective items $X_{4-6}$. In other words, exogenous variables are those constructs which explain other constructs.

One key advantage of SEM is its ability to simultaneously account for multiple endogenous variables as well as their interconnections (Barclay et al. 1995; Chin 2010; Gefen et al. 2000). Each construct, no matter whether it is an endogenous or exogenous variable requires a separate set of items. The items bridge the gap between the more abstract theoretical construct and the actual empirical measurement as stated in the questionnaire. They therefore allow for a meaningful analysis of the underlying theory (Edwards and Bagozzi 2000; MacKenzie et al. 2011).

According to Churchill (1979) researchers should always employ appropriate theory behind the constructs and their items as well as a proper data collection procedure, i.e. through a suitable questionnaire. Hair et al. (2013, p. 12) define theory as "a set of systematically related hypotheses developed following the scientific method that can be used to explain and predict outcomes". The authors differentiate between measurement theory and structural theory.

Structural theory, on the one hand, refers to the relationship between the latent variables. This theory is developed from the researcher's collective knowledge, i.e. through accumulating real-life data or by discussing existing literature and the theoretical ideas used therein, both of which also form the basis for the model developed on the 'eGK' as later shown. Measurement theory, on the other hand, is concerned with the actual measurement of the latent variables. These can be measured either in a reflective or a formative way, with the terms describing the nature of the relationship between a construct and its variables (MacKenzie et al. 2011). In the above theoretical depiction, $Y_1$ is measured in a formative way with the arrows pointing towards the construct, while $Y_3$ is measured in a reflective way with arrows pointing towards the individual items. Reflective items have an error term associated with them, i.e. $e_7$ or $e_{12}$ in the theoretical path model depiction, while formative items are considered as being error free (Diamantopoulos 2011; Hair et al. 2013).

Figure 6.2 further demonstrates the difference between measuring a construct using reflective versus formative measurements. Cenfetelli and Bassellier (2009) describe the key difference between the two as its reversed causality. As the names suggest, reflective items are a reflection of their construct while formative items

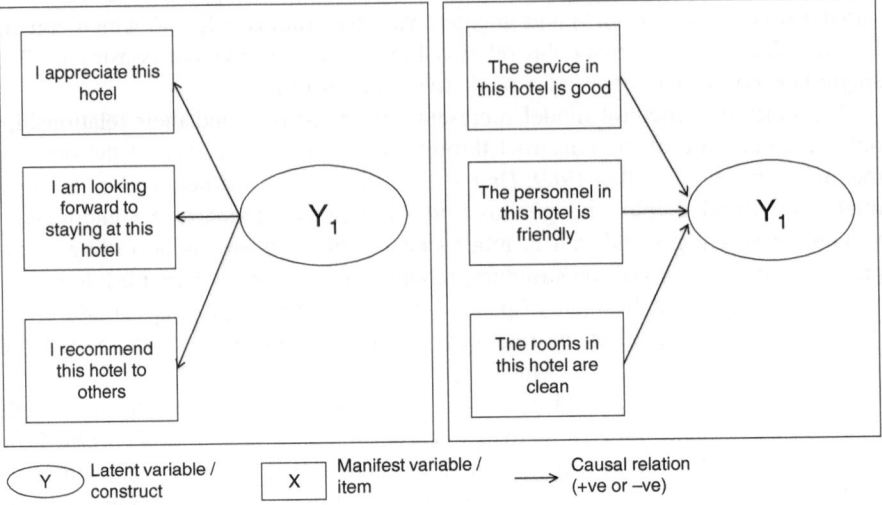

**Fig. 6.2** Satisfaction as a formative and reflective construct. *Note* Adapted from Albers in Esposito Vinzi et al. (2010) and Hair et al. (2013)

collectively form or shape their construct (Petter et al. 2007). The example depicted in Fig. 6.2 therefore shows how "satisfaction with a hotel" can be considered from both ways (Albers 2010; Hair et al. 2013). Hair et al. (2013, p. 45) suggest that using reflective measures is more appropriate in cases where researchers want to "test theories with respect to satisfaction". A formative approach would be better suited to a case where a researcher wants to determine the most important drivers of satisfaction. The decision which of the two measures to use has been subject to debate, with a number of authors providing further criteria for doing so (Chin 1998; Diamantopoulos and Winklhofer 2001; Jarvis et al. 2003; Rossiter 2002). Finally, beyond pure data-driven perspectives theoretical considerations should additionally be considered when making the decision between using formative or reflective measures.

Another famous example explaining the difference between reflective and formative measurements is the one of "drunkenness" as otherwise discussed by Backhaus et al. (2010) and Chin (1998).

### 6.1.2  Covariance Versus Variance-Based Structural Equation Models

While structural equation modeling is regarded as a quasi-standard, it is important to differentiate between two approaches to calculating relationships in a structural equation model: the covariance-based approach (CB-SEM) and the variance-based partial least squares approach (PLS-SEM) (Hair et al. 2011b, 2013). Both approaches integrate the outer and inner models (see Fig. 6.1), to simultaneously assess both this integrated measurement and the structural model (Gefen et al. 2011). Furthermore, both approaches rely on different characteristics and therefore entail a number of advantages and disadvantages in analyzing data.

PLS-SEM is estimated through an ordinary least squares regression-based method (OLS). CB-SEM by contrast is based on a maximum likelihood procedure (ML) [please refer to the following for detailed discussions on CB-SEM: Homburg and Baumgartner (1995) and Homburg (1992)]. PLS-SEM uses data available to estimate coefficients, i.e. the relationships in the path model, which in turn maximize the $R^2$ value of the endogenous variable. It therefore aims at minimizing the error terms, in other words the variance, of the endogenous variable (Hair et al. 2013). For this reason PLS-SEM is regarded as predictive in nature while it is also referred to as the variance-based approach to structural equation modeling. It should furthermore be noted that PLS-SEM is similar but not equivalent to PLS regression given that it relies on the specified relationships between the latent variables as well as with respect to their items (Hair et al. 2013; Mateos-Aparicio 2011).

Since developed by Wold (1975) and further extended by Lohmöller (1989) PLS-SEM has in recent years gained momentum as a tool for analysis given its predictive features, its ability to also work with smaller sample sizes as well as more relaxed requirements regarding the underlying data (Cassel et al. 1999; Dijkstra 2010; Jöreskog and Wold 1982). PLS-SEM can furthermore deal with reflective, formative and single-item constructs and is therefore applicable to an array of different research questions.

However, a choice between the CB-SEM and PLS-SEM should be motivated by a number of factors beyond these general advantages of PLS-SEM. Hair et al. (2011b), (2013) and Gefen et al. (2011) provide a number of criteria which can serve as a rule of thumb towards making such a choice. Table 6.1 summarizes these:

Given these criteria PLS-SEM was chosen to analyze both the quantitative data gathered during the Pilot Study of Phase I as well as the data for the main study in Phase III. Gefen et al. (2011) have argued that PLS-SEM is particularly applicable in cases where the study builds on rich data, as is the case in this study. Besides, when the nature of the analysis is such as to understand the relationships between constructs, i.e. when research is still in its early stages, rather than measure the magnitude of those relationships, PLS-SEM arguably better suited than CB-SEM (Goodhue et al. 2012). Since this study is the first to measure the effect of societal forces on user resistance, forces which have previously been associated mainly with user acceptance theory, this type of analysis is particularly applicable. Finally, Goodhue et al. (2012) also found that PLS' power and ability to identify false positives is equal to that of other analysis techniques.

**Table 6.1** Selection criteria for PLS-SEM versus CB-SEM

| PLS-SEM | CB-SEM |
|---|---|
| *Research goal* | |
| If the goal is predicting key target constructs or identifying key "driver" constructs, select PLS-SEM | If the goal is theory testing, theory confirmation, or comparison of alternative theories, select CB-SEM |
| If the research is exploratory or an extension of an existing structural theory, select PLS-SEM | |
| *Measurement model specification* | |
| If formative constructs are part of the structural model, select PLS-SEM | Note that formative measures can also be used with CB-SEM but to do so requires accounting for relatively complex and limiting specification rules |
| | If error terms require additional specification, such as covariation, select CB-SEM |
| *Structural model* | |
| If the structural model is complex (many constructs and many indicators), select PLS-SEM | If the model is nonrecursive, select CB-SEM |
| *Data characteristics and algorithm* | |
| If the sample size is relatively low, select PLS-SEM. With large data sets, CB-SEM and PLS-SEM results are similar, provided that a large number of indicator variables are used to measure the latent constructs (consistency at large) | If your data meet the CB-SEM assumptions exactly, for example, with respect to the minimum sample size and the distributional assumptions, select CB-SEM; otherwise, PLS-SEM is a good approximation of CB-SEM results |
| PLS-SEM minimum sample size should be equal to the larger of the following: (1) ten times the largest number of formative indicators used to measure one construct or (2) ten times the largest number of structural paths directed at a particular latent construct in the structural model | |
| If CB-SEM requirements cannot be met (i.e., model specification, identification, nonconvergence, data distributional assumptions), use PLS-SEM as a good approximation of CB-SEM results | If the data are to some extent nonnormal, use PLS-SEM; otherwise, under normal data conditions, CB-SEM and PLS-SEM results are highly similar, with CB-SEM providing slightly more precise model estimates |
| | CB-SEM and PLS-SEM results should be similar. If not, check the model specification to ensure that CB-SEM was appropriately applied. If not, PLS-SEM results are a good approximation of CB-SEM results |
| *Model evaluation* | |
| If you need to use latent variable scores in subsequent analyses, PLS-SEM is the best approach | If your research requires a global goodness-of-fit criterion, then CB-SEM is the preferred approach |
| | If you need to test for measurement model invariance, use CB-SEM |

*Note* Adapted from Hair et al. (2011b), (2013) and Gefen et al. (2011)

## 6.2  Model Development

Given the nature of the factors extracted from the qualitative data in Phase II this research proceeds by explaining user resistance through the lens of perceived isomorphic forces, as already hinted at in the introduction to this thesis. These forces are decomposed according to the stakeholders enacting them, as identified in Table 5.1 in Sect. 5.3. Finally, the effects of data privacy concerns are considered in order to develop an overall model suited to explaining physicians' resistance to eHealth technologies.

As mentioned at the beginning of the thesis, the relevant literature explains isomorphic forces in the form of coercive, mimetic and normative pressures (Currie 2012; DiMaggio and Powell 1983; Mignerat and Rivard 2012). To briefly recapitulate:

*Coercive pressure* is formal and informal pressure exerted on organizations by other organizations on which they are dependent as well as by cultural expectations in the society within which this organization functions (DiMaggio and Powell 1983). With regard to the pressures exerted on German physicians, as observed in the qualitative data and summarized in Table 5.1, perceived coercive would correspond to *'formal pressure'*.

*Mimetic pressure* is the tendency to imitate the actions of structurally equal organizations perceived as successful. In Table 5.1, mimetic pressure corresponds to *'following others' examples'*.

*Normative pressure* is described as "members of an organizational field such as suppliers, customers, consultants, and the government ...promote various features of the product (Swanson and Ramiller 1997), thus shaping institutional norms regarding implementation and consequent assimilation of [IS] systems" (Liang et al. 2007, p. 66). In Table 5.1, it therefore corresponds to *'setting new standards'*.

Daniels et al. (2002) argue that perceived isomorphic forces influence individuals' behavior through their mental model of the organizational field. This is of particular importance as the ultimate users of eHealth technologies are not the government or hospital management often responsible for the rollout, but the individual doctors, be it in their own practice or within a hospital. Jensen et al. (2009, p. 345) go on to argue that "institutional pressures are normally exerted from the society and organizational field on organizations and individuals as a top-down process". Finally, "it is therefore important to examine the content of institutional logics, by investigating the specific belief systems as they are understood and interpreted by field members" (Currie and Guah 2007, p. 237; Scott 2001).

The behavior of individual doctors gains further significance as physicians in Germany normally run their own medical practice, hence representing the organization itself. Venkatesh et al. (2011, p. 524) argue that "this is important because firm-level benefits are ultimately garnered when individuals in critical roles in healthcare organizations embrace and use implemented systems and, if such individual use occurs, contribute to positive outcomes".

Finally, isomorphic forces are shown to have a direct link to user resistance behavior. Oliver (1991) illustrates that isomorphic pressures may lead to an engagement in defensive action while Currie and Guah (2007) point out that doctors perceive their key task as treating patients, not to perform administrative tasks. eHealth technologies which require them to increasingly do the latter might not fit their self-perceived professional role leading to user resistance.

## 6.3 Hypotheses

As Liang et al. (2007, p. 61) state, "external forces, no matter how strong they are, will have no effect on the behavior of an organization without first affecting the behavior of human agents within the organization". External factors can therefore be seen as directly influencing individual user behavior as individuals internalize the information obtained from others. For example, a colleague's positive opinion can reduce a user's uncertainty over new information systems and decrease perceived switching costs associated with this system (Burnkrant and Cousineau 1975; Kim and Kankanhalli 2009). This argument about the internalization of information also holds as users internalize the information they receive from outside an organization i.e. through isomorphic forces such as the opinion of the broader public.

Following Liang et al. (2007) *coercive pressure* is defined as formal and informal pressures perceived by virtue of a number of relevant stakeholders. The approach suggested by Taylor and Todd (1995) is taken to decompose the construct of coercive pressure according to its individual stakeholders. This is further confirmed by the data analyzed in Phase II of this research. As such, monolithic belief structures, otherwise containing a variety of dimensions, can be broken up. They will hence become clearer and can be interpreted individually (Taylor and Todd 1995). Increasing perceived coercive pressure will influences a user to switch to a new system. Given the various stakeholders identified in Phase II, perceived coercive pressure from the government, the umbrella organization of payors, the general public and competitive conditions are accounted for. Thus:

> *H1-4: Increased coercive force [by stakeholder] has a negative effect on user resistance.*

*Mimetic pressure*, defined as the "perceived extent to which competitors have benefitted from the assimilating [to the technology]", will affect user behavior as users want to imitate the perceived success of their competitors (Liang et al. 2007, p. 68; Teo et al. 2003). Affirmative mimetic pressure will therefore drive the user to imitate their competitors and adopt a new technology. As one interviewee in the qualitative study stated: *"Of course some doctors already work in local networks today. They talk about the advantages of electronic patient files"*. Hence:

*H5: Increased mimetic force has a negative effect on user resistance.*

Like in Liang et al. (2007, p. 68) *normative pressure* is defined as "the perceived extent to which members from the dyadic relational channels have adopted [the new technology] and the extent the government [...] promote the use of information technology". In the context of the case of the 'eGK' technology these dyadic rational channels can for example be comprised of the medical technology industry or the patients. A member of the medical technology industry interviewed in Phase II states: *"In 2010, the industry issued an initiative to draw attention to a re-evaluation of the technology"*. Indeed, this very much suggests their promotion of the technology. The construct of perceived normative pressure is furthermore decomposed according to the stakeholders identified from the qualitative data analyzed in Phase II. As such, it is hypothesized that perceived affirmative, normative pressure by medical technology providers, patients and the government will drive physicians towards using the technology. The medical technology providers could therefore arguably represent what Liang et al. (2007) define as suppliers, while patients could be related to their concept of customers. However, it should be noted that the physicians themselves should be considered the customers of the 'eGK' technology in accordance with other authors who have argued that doctors effectively employ such eHealth technology (Currie 2012):

*H6-8: Increased normative force [by stakeholder] has a negative effect on user resistance.*

Featherman and Pavlou (2003) describe *perceived data privacy risk* as the potential loss of control over personal information expressed through additional uncertainties or potential dangers associated with the use of information systems. Especially Internet services are perceived as unsecure. Perceived privacy risk is therefore made up of a combination of uncertainty, i.e. the probability of a loss, as well as danger, i.e. the cost of this loss, and has a negative effect on the adoption of new information systems (Dowling and Staelin 1994). Given that medical data in association with the 'eGK' technology is exchanged through the Internet, it is argued that doctors will perceive the technology as risky. One doctor interviewed formulated his distrust as follows: *"The technology is not secure. Would people finally believe this if information was leaked and it was found out that a famous politician has HIV?"*. Thus:

*H9: Data privacy risk has a positive effect on user resistance.*

Figure 6.3 depicts the research model and the hypotheses:

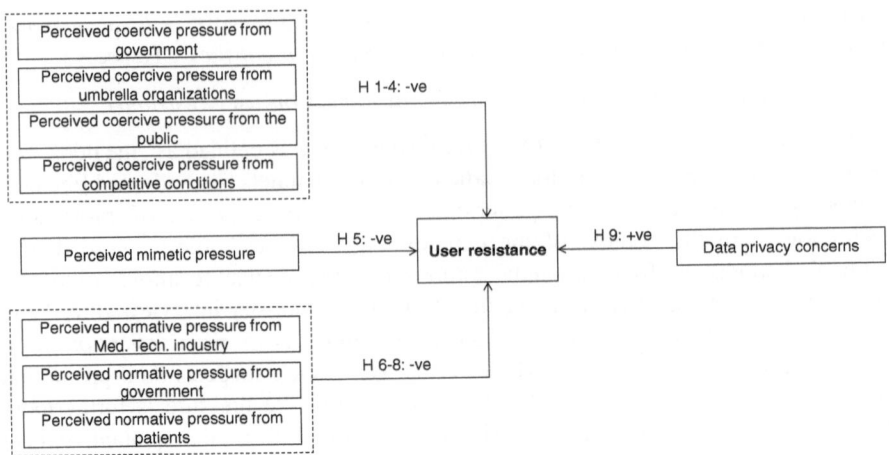

**Fig. 6.3** Research model and hypotheses

## 6.4  Instrument Validation

### 6.4.1  Construct Conceptualization

While the research model of this quantitative study is conceptualized on the basis of the findings from the qualitative data and the literature previously discussed, it is important to note that subsequently all constructs used in this study have effectively been taken from already existing literature within the field of information systems research.

Therefore, user resistance is measured by drawing on the construct and measures of Kim and Kankanhalli (2009) as already described in Phase I.

For the measures of perceived coercive and normative pressure this study builds on Liang et al. (2007). The authors draw on the idea of isomorphic forces in the context of institutional theory. The effects of such isomorphic forces have been discussed in various information systems context, also in the context of eHealth as previously described in Sect. 3.3. For mimetic pressure this study builds on Liang et al. (2007) as well as Teo et al. (2003). For reasons of consistency with the questionnaire, all items were placed on a seven-point Likert scale as opposed to the five-point scale used by Liang et al. (2007).

The measures of perceived data privacy risk are based on the measures by Featherman and Pavlou (2003) and Wunderlich (2013). Additionally, an exploratory factor analysis with VARIMAX rotation was performed. The particular result highlighted one construct with five items, three of which have otherwise also been associated with data security concerns and two of which have been associated with data privacy concerns. The results are consistent with Wunderlich (2013).

Table 6.2 provides a detailed overview over the constructs and measures used as well as their literary sources:

**Table 6.2** Final list of constructs and items used

| Construct | Item | Source[a] |
|---|---|---|
| User resistance | I will not comply with the change to the new way of working with the 'eGK' | Authors based on Kim and Kankanhalli (2009) |
| | I oppose the change to the new way of working with the 'eGK' | |
| | I refuse to accept the change to the new way of working with the 'eGK' | |
| Coercive pressure by govt. | The government requires me to use the 'eGK' | Liang et al. (2007) |
| | I feel pressure from the government, to use the 'eGK' in the future | Authors based on related scales from Liang et al. (2007) |
| | The Ministry of Health tries to make me use the 'eGK' | |
| Coercive pressure by payor org. | The lead associations of the payor organizations require me to use the 'eGK' | Authors based on related scales from Liang et al. (2007) |
| | I feel pressure from the lead associations of the payor organizations to use the 'eGK' in the future | |
| | I feel growing pressure from the lead associations of the payor organizations to quickly implement the 'eGK' | |
| | The lead associations of the payor organizations employ all means available to put me under pressure to use the 'eGK' in the future | |
| Coercive pressure by public | I feel pressure from the general public to use the 'eGK' in the future | Authors based on related scales from Liang et al. (2007) |
| | I feel public pressure to use the 'eGK' in the future | |
| | The media puts pressure on me to use the 'eGK' in the future | |
| Coercive pressure by comp. condition | The competitive conditions require me to use the 'eGK' | Liang et al. (2007) |
| | I feel pressure due to competitive conditions to use the 'eGK' in the future | Authors based on related scales from Liang et al. (2007) |
| | In the long run I will only remain competitive if I use the 'eGK' | |
| | The competitive conditions push me towards changing to the 'eGK' | |
| Mimetic pressure | Our competitors who will adopt the 'eGK' will greatly benefit | Liang et al. (2007), Teo et al. (2003) |
| | Our competitors who will adopt the 'eGK' are favorably perceived by the industry as well as patients | |
| | Our competitors who will adopt the 'eGK' will be more competitive | Chen (2013) |

(continued)

**Table 6.2** (continued)

| Construct | Item | Source[a] |
|---|---|---|
| Normative pressure by Med-Tech. industry | The industry supports the adoption of the 'eGK' | Liang et al. (2007) |
| | The medical technology industry endorses the adoption of the 'eGK' | Authors based on related scales from Liang et al. (2007) |
| | Medical technology providers are in favor of the 'eGK' technology | |
| Normative pressure by patients | My patients want to use the 'eGK' | Authors based on related scales from Liang et al. (2007) |
| | My patients speak positively about the 'eGK' | |
| | My patients believe in the advantages of the 'eGK' | |
| | My patients support the introduction of the 'eGK' | |
| Normative pressure by govt. | The extent to which the government promotes the 'eGK' influences me to use the 'eGK' | Liang et al. (2007) |
| | The government supports the adoption of the 'eGK' | |
| | The norms set by the government encourage me to use the 'eGK' | Authors based on related scales from Liang et al. (2007) |
| Data privacy concerns | I am worried about the data security of the 'eGK' technology | Featherman and Pavlou (2003); Wunderlich (2013) |
| | Internet hackers might take control of my patient data if I were to use the 'eGK' technology | |
| | Data security in the context of the 'eGK' technology is not ensured | |
| | Using the 'eGK' could lead to a loss of control over my personal patient data | |
| | Using the 'eGK' could lead to a loss of my privacy because my patients' data could be used without my knowledge | |
| Behavioral intention | I intend to use the 'eGK' in the next years | Venkatesh et al. (2003) |
| | I plan to use the 'eGK' in the next years | |
| | I plan to use the 'eGK' on a daily basis | Wunderlich (2013) |
| | I can envision employing the possibilities of the 'eGK' within the practice | |

[a]All items were jointly developed based on both the qualitative data obtained in Phase II of this research as well as the relevant literature (this table lists the literary sources)

Given that all constructs build on existing theory the authors of which have employed reflective items, the items in this study are measured as reflective items too. Where applicable, items were added to create a better contextual fit to the study.

Finally, the measures of the socio-demographic, i.e. control variables, were developed together with industry experts who have proven their expertise as they regularly send out questionnaires to physicians on the topic of information systems within the healthcare field. These items were measured as single-item reflective measures (overview in Table A.4 of the Appendix).

Given that the 'eGK' technology is not yet fully rolled out and that not all physicians might therefore be aware of the various technological and logistical details of this eHealth program, all participants were presented with a short introductory text which ensured sufficient understanding to answer the questions amongst the participants of the survey (please also refer to Figs. A.1 and A.2 in the Appendix).

## 6.4.2 Scale Development

The relevant literature has stressed the importance of ensuring both content and face validity when distributing measures to potential respondents (DeVellis 2003; Moore and Benbasat 1991; Nunnally and Bernstein 1994). Face validity therefore assesses whether an item actually measures what it is intended to measure. Content validity assesses the degree to which the items suitably represent the theoretical content of their respective construct. In other words, if one imagines a dartboard, face validity is ensured if the darts do not miss the board while content validity is ensured if the board is equally covered as opposed to darts only hitting certain areas. This implies that items should not be too similar.

Following the suggestions by DeVellis (2003) and Moore and Benbasat (1991) the items were therefore presented to two independent panels of judges in two rounds. The first panel consisted of scholars who have expertise in conducting quantitative research. The second panel consisted of practitioners familiar with the subject of the 'eGK' technology implementation program. The judges were presented with a list of items and constructs. They were then asked to sort the items, which were randomly listed, into those categories that best represented the implied constructs. Two rounds of such sorting were conducted and items were dropped or rephrased until a proper fit was ensured. Overall, and as expected given that the items were largely inferred from previously tested measures, an appropriate fit was ensured quickly.

Just as in Phase I of the research, the items were again translated into German so that all participants could answer in their mother tongue. They were also rephrased to fit the subject of the 'eGK' system to further ensure content and face validity (Moore and Benbasat 1991).

Likert scales were used to measure the items. This is a common methodology and frequently employed in behavioral research (Hinkin 1998). Except for the control variables, all items for all constructs were placed on a seven-point Liker scale ranging from "I disagree" to "I agree". Equidistance was hence ensured.

### 6.4.3 Pilot Study

Moore and Benbasat (1991) have suggested that constructs and items should be tested before the actual survey is conducted. A pilot study was indeed performed, which is the study described in Phase I as discussed in Chap. 4. A number of constructs were later added to the final questionnaire of the larger study in Phase III. Although these were therefore not tested anymore, they are based on existing theoretical constructs and items previously verified by other researchers. As displayed in Chap. 4, the pilot study provided adequate results meeting all necessary evaluation criteria.

### 6.4.4 Sample and Data Collection Procedure

Given that the goal of this main quantitative study is to empirically test for the influence of isomorphic forces on the resistance of German doctors to the 'eGK' technology, both a large as well as representative sample was aimed for. Data was thus collected through a broad field study involving doctors who practice medicine in Germany and who will be supplied with the 'eGK' technology. Just as in the empirical test conducted in Phase I, the data was collected using an online survey distributed to German doctors of different specializations across the whole country.

Making use of an online survey had several advantages. Firstly, it allowed for including a brief introductory text, which ensured that all participants had the required information to answer the questions posed (see Figs. A.1 and A.2 in the Appendix). Furthermore, researchers were thus able to provide detailed information about the study including easy-access contact information such as email which many participants made use of to reply and elaborate on their opinion towards the 'eGK' technology. Moreover, the functionality of the online survey made it possible to observe whether participants correctly read through the questions or just skimmed through the answers. The questionnaire was also designed so that participants were forced to answer all questions before proceeding to the next page. Finally, it allowed for reaching a large number of physicians of various specializations and from across the whole of the country.

Like in Phase I, the email addresses of the physicians were purchased from the same specialized provider ensuring a representative sample across profession (for example general practitioner, surgeon, oculist etc.), gender and region. In total, 707 doctors responded to the questionnaire, out of which 398 doctors answered the questionnaire in full. Only those questionnaires were used to test the hypotheses of the model. The data used to test the hypotheses of the research model therefore did not contain any missing data, also thanks to the force-answer function of the online survey, so that there was no need to employ software tools to handle such missing data (Ringle et al. 2005).

During the data collection procedure the researchers were approached by an online publishing house which had heard about the research initiative through participants in the survey. The online publishing house offered to post a link to out the questionnaire via their website. Another 71 fully answered questionnaires were collected through this channel.

To evaluate the possibility of response bias it was examined how well the data represented the German population of doctors. The average respondent was between 45 and 59 years old corresponding to the average age of doctors in Germany. Overall, doctors of more than 20 specializations participated in the survey, of which approximately 45 % were general practitioners. Importantly all doctors answered themselves, none had their receptionist answer for them. 82 % of the 469 doctors were male.

## 6.5 Analysis

Smart PLS Version 2.0.M3 was used to analyze the data (Ringle et al. 2005). This selection is in line with recent methodological choices within the information systems discipline on the use of partial least squares analysis versus other analysis techniques such as regression or structural equation modeling (Gefen and Straub 2005; Ringle et al. 2012).

Typically, PLS-SEM models are assessed in two stages, the first being the analysis of the "reliability and validity of the measurement model" and the second being the analysis of the structural model itself (Hulland 1999, p. 198).

### 6.5.1 Assessment of Measurement Model

In order to test the validity of the research model a number of tests were performed that are recommended by researchers in the field, who also use partial least squares analysis (Brown and Venkatesh 2005; Chin 1998; Gefen and Straub 2005; Hulland 1999). The results are summarized below.

Firstly, content validity, i.e. whether the items reflect the universal content of the instrument, was ensured through a thorough literature review as described in Chap. 3 of this research as well as through the review of expert judges as described in Sect. 6.4.2.

Secondly, internal consistency reliability within the model should be confirmed through the measure of composite reliability which "takes into account the outer loadings of the indicator variables" (Hair et al. 2013, p. 101). The measure of composite reliability varies between 0 and 1 and higher values are more desirable. Hulland (1999) suggest that the composite reliabilities of the constructs should be greater than 0.70 which very much was the case for the data.

Thirdly, convergent validity, i.e. "the extent to which a measure correlates positively with alternative measures of the same construct" is to be evaluated (Hair et al. 2013, p. 102). One way of doing this is to measure the average variance extracted (AVE) at the construct level. AVE, also described as the communality of the construct, is the overall mean of the squared loadings of the items associated with the construct and is measured by taking the sum of the squared loadings and dividing them by the number of indicators. The AVE for each construct should be greater than 0.50, which suggests that the construct explains more than 50 % of the variance of its items (Bhattacherjee and Premkumar 2004). Again these criteria are met by the data, see Table 6.3.

Another way to measure convergent validity is to assess the outer loadings of the items onto their respective constructs. Higher loadings therefore suggest that the items have a lot in common and that this effect is in turn captured by the construct with the threshold of the loading often described as being 0.70 or above (Gefen and Straub 2005). As shown in Table 6.4 this criterion holds. Besides, all outer loadings of the items onto their respective constructs were significant.

Furthermore, discriminant validity should be established. Discriminant validity measures whether a construct is in fact distinct from the other constructs within the model. One common way of assessing this is by looking at the cross loadings of the individual items (Gefen and Straub 2005; Götz et al. 2010). One therefore observes whether the outer loadings of the items are greater with respect to their associated construct than with respect to the other constructs, which would be a case of cross loading. In other words, if cross loadings on other constructs exist discriminant validity might arise. However, this is not the case in this model as shown in Table 6.5.

**Table 6.3** Cronbach alphas, composite reliabilities and AVEs (main model)

| Construct | Cronbach alpha | Composite reliabilities | AVE |
|---|---|---|---|
| Age | 1 | 1 | 1 |
| Coercive pressure comp. conditions | 0.927 | 0.940 | 0.798 |
| Coercive pressure government | 0.846 | 0.905 | 0.761 |
| Coercive pressure public opinion | 0.896 | 0.932 | 0.822 |
| Coercive pressure umbrella org. | 0.924 | 0.946 | 0.814 |
| Data privacy concerns | 0.891 | 0.920 | 0.696 |
| Internet | 1 | 1 | 1 |
| KV-SafeNet | 1 | 1 | 1 |
| Mimetic pressure | 0.842 | 0.903 | 0.756 |
| Normative pressure government | 0.936 | 0.959 | 0.885 |
| Normative pressure Med-Tech. industry | 0.952 | 0.959 | 0.885 |
| Normative pressure patients | 0.920 | 0.943 | 0.806 |
| User resistance | 0.879 | 0.925 | 0.805 |
| Size of practice | 1 | 1 | 1 |

*Note* Age, internet, KV-SafeNet and size of practice are control variables

**Table 6.4** Item means and standard deviations, outer loadings and their statistical significance (main model)

| Item | Mean | Standard deviation | Outer loading | T statistics ($|O/STERR|$) |
|---|---|---|---|---|
| User resistance item RTC1 | 4.966 | 2.326 | 0.909 | 73.234 |
| User resistance item RTC3 | 5.380 | 2.105 | 0.875 | 56.999 |
| User resistance item RTC5 | 4.535 | 2.362 | 0.908 | 77.304 |
| Coercive pressure item CP1a | 5.454 | 1.869 | 0.805 | 24.045 |
| Coercive pressure item CP1c | 5.729 | 1.879 | 0.902 | 57.562 |
| Coercive pressure item CP1e | 5.751 | 1.762 | 0.905 | 72.209 |
| Coercive pressure item CP2a | 5.770 | 1.760 | 0.874 | 41.046 |
| Coercive pressure item CP2b | 5.765 | 1.812 | 0.918 | 73.709 |
| Coercive pressure item CP2c | 5.840 | 1.681 | 0.905 | 69.139 |
| Coercive pressure item CP2d | 5.672 | 1.788 | 0.911 | 74.989 |
| Coercive pressure item CP3b | 3.045 | 2.099 | 0.908 | 16.817 |
| Coercive pressure item CP3c | 3.328 | 2.148 | 0.877 | 15.988 |
| Coercive pressure item CP3d | 3.446 | 2.101 | 0.924 | 36.178 |
| Coercive pressure item CP4a | 2.582 | 1.988 | 0.919 | 27.279 |
| Coercive pressure item CP4b | 2.725 | 2.071 | 0.818 | 14.039 |
| Coercive pressure item CP4d | 2.810 | 2.097 | 0.926 | 46.392 |
| Coercive pressure item CP4e | 2.595 | 1.951 | 0.907 | 22.974 |
| Mimetic pressure item MP1 | 2.761 | 1.760 | 0.873 | 40.160 |
| Mimetic pressure item MP3 | 2.392 | 1.531 | 0.878 | 51.398 |
| Mimetic pressure item MP7 | 2.497 | 1.737 | 0.858 | 33.152 |
| Normative pressure item NOP1a | 5.655 | 1.681 | 0.941 | 5.259 |
| Normative pressure item NOP1b | 5.588 | 1.689 | 0.983 | 4.909 |
| Normative pressure item NOP1c | 5.578 | 1.730 | 0.897 | 4.524 |
| Normative pressure item NOP2a | 2.143 | 1.458 | 0.893 | 46.535 |
| Normative pressure item NOP2b | 1.857 | 1.256 | 0.901 | 46.902 |
| Normative pressure item NOP2c | 2.006 | 1.398 | 0.901 | 51.415 |
| Normative pressure item NOP2d | 1.964 | 1.367 | 0.895 | 37.848 |
| Normative pressure item NOP3a | 6.009 | 1.384 | 0.944 | 56.249 |
| Normative pressure item NOP3b | 6.021 | 1.360 | 0.936 | 73.697 |
| Normative pressure item NOP3d | 6.036 | 1.416 | 0.943 | 49.110 |
| Data privacy concerns item PDSR1 | 6.151 | 1.675 | 0.860 | 41.099 |
| Data privacy concerns item PDSR2 | 6.019 | 1.592 | 0.799 | 26.632 |
| Data privacy concerns item PDSR4 | 5.959 | 1.762 | 0.835 | 29.201 |
| Data privacy concerns items PPR1 | 5.804 | 1.863 | 0.876 | 51.986 |
| Data privacy concerns item PPR2 | 5.789 | 1.849 | 0.799 | 28.751 |

**Table 6.5** Cross loadings of items in the sample (main model)

| | Age | CP comp conditions | CP govt. | CP public opinion | CP umbrella Org. | Data security | Internet | KV-SafeNet | MP | NOP govt. | NP MedTech | NP patients | Resistance | Size of practice |
|---|---|---|---|---|---|---|---|---|---|---|---|---|---|---|
| Age | **1.000** | 0.030 | 0.053 | 0.074 | 0.071 | 0.019 | -0.040 | -0.049 | -0.033 | 0.054 | 0.094 | -0.001 | 0.107 | -0.134 |
| CP 1a | 0.036 | 0.107 | **0.805** | 0.170 | 0.515 | 0.242 | 0.077 | 0.100 | -0.083 | 0.368 | 0.083 | -0.142 | 0.242 | -0.026 |
| CP 1c | 0.071 | 0.013 | **0.902** | 0.288 | 0.672 | 0.457 | 0.133 | 0.052 | -0.172 | 0.368 | 0.149 | -0.245 | 0.372 | -0.003 |
| CP 1e | 0.031 | -0.072 | **0.905** | 0.204 | 0.614 | 0.407 | 0.111 | 0.139 | -0.242 | 0.424 | 0.181 | -0.277 | 0.402 | 0.026 |
| CP 2a | 0.061 | 0.027 | 0.624 | 0.241 | **0.874** | 0.346 | 0.121 | 0.137 | -0.194 | 0.341 | 0.119 | -0.207 | 0.298 | -0.061 |
| CP 2b | 0.053 | 0.020 | 0.670 | 0.339 | **0.918** | 0.448 | 0.172 | 0.094 | -0.210 | 0.283 | 0.171 | -0.226 | 0.360 | -0.031 |
| CP 2c | 0.062 | -0.044 | 0.613 | 0.307 | **0.905** | 0.443 | 0.162 | 0.149 | -0.240 | 0.305 | 0.148 | -0.256 | 0.350 | -0.088 |
| CP 2d | 0.080 | 0.005 | 0.603 | 0.314 | **0.911** | 0.469 | 0.181 | 0.100 | -0.216 | 0.246 | 0.113 | -0.242 | 0.373 | -0.065 |
| CP 3b | 0.071 | 0.308 | 0.187 | **0.908** | 0.252 | 0.160 | 0.039 | 0.000 | 0.199 | 0.114 | 0.128 | 0.104 | 0.123 | -0.016 |
| CP 3c | 0.047 | 0.292 | 0.249 | **0.887** | 0.302 | 0.163 | 0.058 | 0.032 | 0.189 | 0.162 | 0.144 | 0.117 | 0.102 | -0.047 |
| CP 3d | 0.077 | 0.245 | 0.258 | **0.924** | 0.343 | 0.231 | 0.112 | 0.074 | 0.135 | 0.173 | 0.171 | 0.051 | 0.181 | -0.016 |
| CP 4a | 0.036 | **0.919** | 0.057 | 0.316 | 0.077 | -0.107 | -0.153 | -0.138 | 0.511 | 0.057 | 0.082 | 0.217 | -0.157 | -0.056 |
| CP 4b | 0.120 | **0.818** | 0.124 | 0.471 | 0.150 | -0.015 | -0.065 | -0.080 | 0.419 | 0.056 | 0.109 | 0.174 | -0.072 | -0.084 |
| CP 4d | -0.012 | **0.926** | -0.091 | 0.167 | -0.122 | -0.275 | -0.173 | -0.192 | 0.568 | 0.056 | 0.046 | 0.304 | -0.288 | -0.010 |
| CP 4e | 0.053 | **0.907** | 0.075 | 0.362 | 0.104 | -0.081 | -0.121 | -0.125 | 0.474 | 0.036 | 0.049 | 0.201 | -0.125 | -0.053 |
| Internet | -0.040 | -0.161 | 0.126 | 0.084 | 0.178 | 0.224 | **1.000** | 0.204 | -0.210 | 0.044 | -0.062 | -0.179 | 0.178 | -0.138 |
| KV SafeNet | -0.049 | -0.168 | 0.112 | 0.045 | 0.131 | 0.072 | 0.204 | **1.000** | -0.169 | 0.123 | 0.042 | -0.069 | 0.166 | -0.061 |
| MP 1 | -0.022 | 0.486 | -0.159 | 0.142 | -0.193 | -0.210 | -0.142 | -0.157 | **0.873** | 0.011 | 0.085 | 0.366 | -0.239 | -0.038 |
| MP 3 | -0.031 | 0.419 | -0.211 | 0.134 | -0.258 | -0.270 | -0.194 | -0.125 | **0.878** | -0.051 | 0.038 | 0.519 | -0.336 | -0.024 |
| MP 7 | -0.031 | 0.612 | -0.147 | 0.214 | -0.153 | -0.188 | -0.208 | -0.167 | **0.858** | 0.001 | 0.094 | 0.384 | -0.248 | -0.002 |
| NOP 1a | 0.088 | 0.069 | 0.125 | 0.178 | 0.134 | 0.131 | -0.075 | 0.031 | 0.079 | 0.300 | **0.941** | 0.038 | 0.044 | 0.076 |
| NOP 1b | 0.093 | 0.065 | 0.180 | 0.151 | 0.156 | 0.121 | -0.052 | 0.047 | 0.074 | 0.379 | **0.983** | 0.066 | 0.082 | 0.079 |

(continued)

**Table 6.5** (continued)

| | Age | CP comp conditions | CP govt. | CP public opinion | CP umbrella Org. | Data security | Internet | KV-SafeNet | MP | NOP govt. | NP MedTech | NP patients | Resistance | Size of practice |
|---|---|---|---|---|---|---|---|---|---|---|---|---|---|---|
| NOP 1c | 0.061 | 0.097 | 0.101 | 0.149 | 0.097 | 0.083 | -0.059 | 0.049 | 0.115 | 0.345 | **0.897** | 0.075 | 0.001 | 0.052 |
| NOP 2a | 0.029 | 0.228 | -0.258 | 0.031 | -0.250 | -0.307 | -0.172 | -0.055 | 0.422 | -0.025 | 0.048 | **0.893** | -0.287 | 0.011 |
| NOP 2b | -0.021 | 0.264 | -0.249 | 0.126 | -0.232 | -0.303 | -0.150 | -0.053 | 0.452 | -0.041 | 0.056 | **0.901** | -0.260 | -0.013 |
| NOP 2c | -0.016 | 0.266 | -0.199 | 0.118 | -0.229 | -0.270 | -0.152 | -0.074 | 0.464 | 0.014 | 0.055 | **0.901** | -0.227 | -0.011 |
| NOP 2d | -0.002 | 0.225 | -0.237 | 0.062 | -0.214 | -0.288 | -0.166 | -0.068 | 0.458 | -0.060 | 0.050 | **0.895** | -0.233 | 0.000 |
| NOP 3a | 0.032 | 0.052 | 0.415 | 0.170 | 0.318 | 0.134 | 0.048 | 0.115 | -0.015 | **0.944** | 0.340 | -0.011 | 0.135 | 0.030 |
| NOP 3b | 0.075 | 0.056 | 0.440 | 0.142 | 0.304 | 0.147 | 0.042 | 0.120 | -0.032 | **0.936** | 0.362 | -0.044 | 0.171 | 0.007 |
| NOP 3d | 0.038 | 0.055 | 0.387 | 0.165 | 0.287 | 0.128 | 0.033 | 0.109 | -0.005 | **0.943** | 0.314 | -0.030 | 0.129 | 0.029 |
| PDSR 1 | 0.000 | -0.192 | 0.315 | 0.179 | 0.357 | **0.860** | 0.176 | 0.016 | -0.246 | 0.096 | 0.118 | -0.302 | 0.406 | -0.078 |
| PDSR 2 | 0.045 | -0.159 | 0.338 | 0.163 | 0.348 | **0.799** | 0.201 | 0.096 | -0.178 | 0.150 | 0.146 | -0.216 | 0.382 | -0.048 |
| PDSR 4 | 0.028 | -0.183 | 0.319 | 0.124 | 0.395 | **0.835** | 0.203 | 0.016 | -0.274 | 0.101 | 0.108 | -0.308 | 0.424 | -0.037 |
| PPR 1 | -0.029 | -0.140 | 0.422 | 0.216 | 0.444 | **0.876** | 0.169 | 0.104 | -0.210 | 0.133 | 0.103 | -0.274 | 0.461 | -0.094 |
| PPR 2 | 0.041 | -0.096 | 0.427 | 0.199 | 0.436 | **0.799** | 0.188 | 0.066 | -0.183 | 0.129 | 0.066 | -0.259 | 0.417 | -0.031 |
| Practice | -0.134 | -0.042 | 0.003 | -0.026 | -0.068 | -0.070 | -0.138 | -0.061 | -0.025 | 0.022 | 0.081 | -0.003 | 0.003 | **1.000** |
| RTC 1 | 0.075 | -0.183 | 0.344 | 0.170 | 0.362 | 0.461 | 0.203 | 0.123 | -0.292 | 0.071 | 0.040 | -0.250 | **0.909** | 0.004 |
| RTC 3 | 0.088 | -0.185 | 0.409 | 0.096 | 0.371 | 0.456 | 0.134 | 0.148 | -0.278 | 0.196 | 0.079 | -0.234 | **0.875** | 0.025 |
| RTC 5 | 0.124 | -0.224 | 0.325 | 0.159 | 0.302 | 0.434 | 0.143 | 0.174 | -0.300 | 0.155 | 0.069 | -0.278 | **0.906** | -0.020 |

Examining the cross loadings has been discussed as a rather liberal measure of testing for discriminant validity (Hair et al. 2011b). Another way of establishing discriminant validity is through the so-called Fornell Larcker criterion which is considered more conservative. The Fornell Larcker criterion is met by ensuring that the square root of AVE of a construct exceeds the correlations between this construct and the other constructs of the model (Bhattacherjee and Premkumar 2004; Fornell and Larcker 1981; Gefen and Straub 2005). As shown in Table 6.6, the square roots of all constructs are larger than the correlation of that construct with others (with the square root of the construct's AVE reported on the main diagonal, the off-diagonal cells showing the correlation between that construct and the others).

Finally, and although composite reliability was already measured, the reliability of the data was also assessed using the measurement of Cronbach Alpha. This is considered a first-generation measurement for determining the reliability of the data as oppose to the second-generation measurements described above. The latter provide a more holistic assessment. A number of authors have suggested that first-generation measurements are inferior given their underlying restrictive assumptions, such as one-dimensionality, and the inability to evaluate measurement errors (Bagozzi and Phillips 1982; Gerbing and Anderson 1988; Homburg and Giering 1996). However, assessing for Cronbach Alpha has also been discussed as a valid measure to test for non-functioning items, particularly when combined with second-generation measurements (Churchill 1979; Homburg and Giering 1996). Cronbach Alpha assumes that reflective items are correlated. Thus, the higher the Cronbach Alpha the higher also the internal consistency within the construct measured. The threshold for a valid Cronbach Alpha is normally described at 0.70 or above which the data surpasses (please refer to Table 6.3).

## 6.5.2 Assessment of the Hypothesized Relationships

As a next step, the hypotheses behind the research model were tested by examining the significance of the parameter estimates. Again Smart PLS 2.0.M3 was used to perform bootstrapping with m = 5000 samples and n = 469 cases. This number of bootstrap samples is both high in general and above the number of cases observed in the data as suggested by Hair et al. (2013). Overall, the model explained 35.2 % of the variance of German physicians' resistance to the 'eGK' technology.

H1 and H3 loaded significantly on user resistance. However, unlike originally hypothesized, perceived coercive pressures from the government and the public had a positive effect on user resistance, ($\beta = +0.164$, $p < 0.05$) and ($\beta = +0.077$, $p < 0.1$) respectively. While H2 was not confirmed at all, the results confirm H4, the negative effect of perceived coercive pressure from competitive conditions on user resistance ($\beta = -0.089$, $p < 0.05$). The model also confirms H5, the negative effect of perceived mimetic pressures on user resistance ($\beta = -0.117$, $p < 0.05$). None of the perceived normative pressures were found to have a significant effect on

**Table 6.6** Square root of AVEs and correlations (main model)

| Construct | 1 | 2 | 3 | 4 | 5 | 6 | 7 | 8 | 9 | 10 | 11 | 12 | 13 | 14 |
|---|---|---|---|---|---|---|---|---|---|---|---|---|---|---|
| Age | **1.000** | | | | | | | | | | | | | |
| CP comp. conditions | 0.030 | **0.893** | | | | | | | | | | | | |
| CP govt. | 0.053 | 0.002 | **0.872** | | | | | | | | | | | |
| CP public opinion | 0.074 | 0.303 | 0.258 | **0.906** | | | | | | | | | | |
| CP umbrella Org. | 0.071 | 0.001 | 0.695 | 0.335 | **0.902** | | | | | | | | | |
| Data privacy | 0.019 | −0.184 | 0.438 | 0.212 | 0.477 | **0.835** | | | | | | | | |
| Internet | −0.040 | −0.161 | 0.126 | 0.084 | 0.178 | 0.224 | **1.000** | | | | | | | |
| KV-SafeNet | −0.049 | −0.168 | 0.112 | 0.045 | 0.131 | 0.072 | 0.204 | **1.000** | | | | | | |
| MP | −0.033 | 0.571 | −0.203 | 0.184 | −0.239 | −0.262 | −0.210 | −0.169 | **0.869** | | | | | |
| NP govt. | 0.054 | 0.058 | 0.443 | 0.167 | 0.322 | 0.146 | 0.044 | 0.123 | −0.020 | **0.941** | | | | |
| NP Med-Tech. | 0.094 | 0.069 | 0.166 | 0.166 | 0.153 | 0.129 | −0.062 | 0.042 | 0.079 | 0.363 | **0.941** | | | |
| NP Patients | −0.001 | 0.273 | −0.264 | 0.092 | −0.259 | −0.327 | −0.179 | −0.069 | 0.499 | −0.032 | 0.058 | **0.898** | | |
| Resistance | 0.107 | −0.220 | 0.401 | 0.157 | 0.385 | 0.502 | 0.178 | 0.166 | −0.323 | 0.157 | 0.070 | −0.283 | **0.897** | |
| Size of practice | −0.134 | −0.042 | 0.003 | −0.026 | −0.068 | −0.070 | −0.138 | −0.061 | −0.025 | 0.022 | 0.081 | −0.003 | 0.003 | **1.000** |

*Note* Square root of AVEs displayed on diagonal; *CP* coercive pressure, *MP* mimetic pressure, *NP* normative pressure

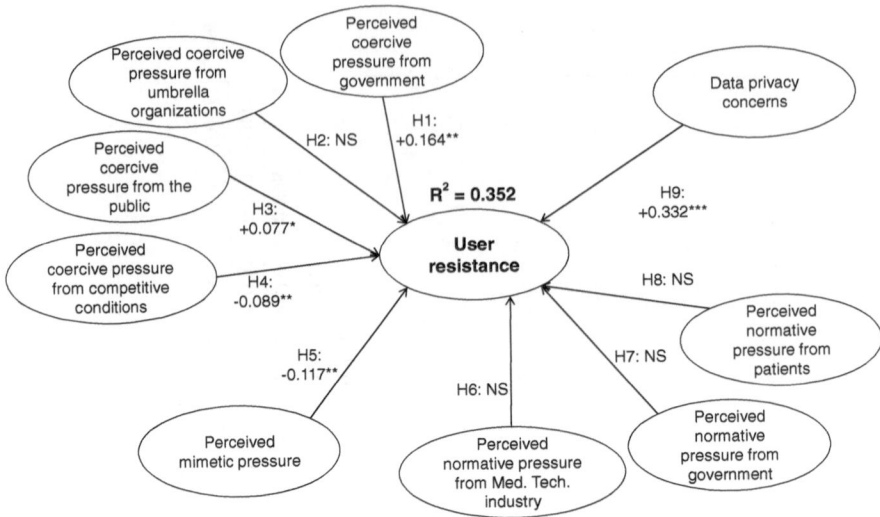

**Fig. 6.4** Results of hypothesis testing (main model). *Note* *** $p < 0.01$; ** $p < 0.05$; * $p < 0.1$; *NS* not significant at 0.1 level

physicians' resistance to the 'eGK' technology. Finally, as suggested by H9, data privacy concerns have a significant effect on user resistance, ($\beta = +0.332, p < 0.001$) (Fig. 6.4).

Besides evaluating the $R^2$ of the model, the effect size of specific omitted constructs on the endogenous variable of user resistance was measured. This effect size is calculated using the formula shown in Fig. 6.5, whereby the effect size of a construct is measured by once computing the $R^2$ of the model including the observed construct and once without.

Cohen (1988) names the thresholds of 0.02, 0.15 and 0.35 as measuring small, medium and large effects. Table 6.7 shows the effect sizes for the exogenous constructs in this model. No changes in the significance of the hypothesized paths of the model were observed as insignificant paths in the research model were also found to have below threshold effect sizes. Only the significant construct of data privacy concerns has a small effect size on the endogenous variable of user resistance.

In order to assess the predictive relevance of the model the so-called Stone-Geisser $Q^2$ value was examined (Geisser 1975; Stone 1974). This criterion evaluates the predictive relevance of PLS-SEM models by forecasting data points of the indicators within reflective measurements of endogenous constructs (Hair et al. 2013; Herrmann et al. 2006). The blindfolding procedure was used to omit every

$$f^2 = (R^2_{included} - R^2_{excluded}) / (1 - R^2_{included})$$

**Fig. 6.5** Formula for calculating the effect size $f^2$

**Table 6.7** Effect size of independent variables on endogenous variable (main model)

| Construct | Relation | Effect size ($f^2$) |
|---|---|---|
| Coercive pressure comp. conditions | Coercive pressure comp. conditions → user resistance | 0.008 |
| Coercive pressure government | Coercive pressure government → user resistance | 0.019 |
| Coercive pressure public opinion | Coercive pressure public opinion → user resistance | 0.008 |
| Coercive pressure umbrella org. | Coercive pressure umbrella org. → user resistance | 0.002 |
| Data privacy concerns | Data privacy concerns → user resistance | 0.113 |
| Mimetic pressure | Mimetic pressure → user resistance | 0.011 |
| Normative pressure government | Normative pressure government → user resistance | 0.000 |
| Normative pressure Med-Tech. industry | Normative pressure Med-Tech. industry → user resistance | 0.002 |
| Normative pressure patients | Normative pressure patients → user resistance | 0.002 |

eighth data point in the endogenous construct's indicators, i.e. the indicators from the construct of user resistance, given that 469 observations were counted. The omission distance D = 8 was chosen so that it would be between 5 and 10 as suggested by Hair et al. (2012) and so that the division of the number of observations used in the model by the distance D is not an integer. The omission distance of D = 8 implies that every eighth data point of the constructs' indicators are deleted in a single round and are subsequently predicted in the blindfolding rounds. In the first predictive round, PLS-SEM estimates are assessed which differ from the original model estimates as well as from the results of the following seven blindfolding rounds. First, the missing values for the reflective endogenous variable are calculated, which together with the predicted outer loadings then allow for a calculation of the other eliminated data points. The following seven blindfolding rounds also follow a similar procedure (Hair et al. 2013).

The actual Stone-Geisser criterion is calculated using the formula displayed in Fig. 6.6. Positive values indicate that the model has predictive relevance for the endogenous construct considered (Fornell and Bookstein 1982; Hair et al. 2013). A $q^2$ value for user resistance of 0.285 was measured confirming the predictive relevance of the structural model.

While assessing the model a number of variables were controlled for, i.e. age of the physicians, the size of their medical practices, whether their practice is already

$$q^2 = (Q^2_{included} - Q^2_{excluded}) / (1 - Q^2_{included})$$

**Fig. 6.6** Formula for calculating Stone-Geisser criterion $q^2$

connected to the Internet and finally whether they are already using a special eHealth system, called KV-SafeNet that allows them to safely connect their practice online to the network of the National Association of Statutory Health Insurance Physicians. As suggested in prior research on PLS analysis, such control variables should be included as independent variables while no hypotheses about their effects are measured (Kock 2011).

About 50 % of the doctors participating in the survey ran their own practice, while 21 % of respondents were part of a legal partnership, but as separate economic entities, and another 19 % of respondents shared a medical partnership also from an economic point of view. Approximately two-thirds of the doctors were connected to the Internet with their practice, while around 54 % also used the KV-SafeNet system. Age was found to have a significant positive effect on user resistance ($\beta = +0.095$, $p < 0.05$) which suggests that older doctors show stronger resistance to the 'eGK' technology than younger ones. This might not come as a surprise given that older physicians might be less comfortable with using information systems in general. In the context of information systems research, Venkatesh et al. (2003) as well as Hall and Mansfield (1975) point to the importance of providing assistance on the job to older workers. In particular, Venkatesh et al. (2003) and Morris and Venkatesh (2000) continue to stress increasing cognitive and physical limitations associated with age in the context of complex information technology implementation.

Furthermore, the use of KV-SafeNet had a significant positive effect on user resistance ($\beta = +0.083$, $p < 0.05$). Given the coding of this variable, this suggests that those doctors that do not yet use the system, show a higher resistance to the 'eGK' technology. Again, this should not come as a surprise.

Concerns about common method variance were addressed taking into account that all of the independent and the dependent variables were measured in one single survey. A test for common method variance was therefore conducted using two separate procedures. First of all, following the recommendations of Podsakoff et al. (2003) anonymity was ensured to all participants in the survey.

Besides, Harman's single-factor test was performed (Podsakoff et al. 2003). Eight factors were found to have an eigenvalue greater than 1. However, there was no general factor emerging in the un-rotated factor solution, which furthermore indicates that common method variance was not a problem.

## 6.6  Discussion of Findings

The goal of this study was to develop a set of tangible variables of societal forces in the context of eHealth and measure their impact on user resistance to new information technologies. The relevant literature has repeatedly suggested that such societal forces impact the behavior of users, especially in the field of eHealth. This notion can, indeed, be supported given the results of this study. As a main lesson learnt, by systematically measuring the effects of perceived isomorphic forces on user resistance, the data importantly suggests: Physicians do not seem to simply reduce their resistance to eHealth because of normative influence. Moreover, they are even harder to push towards using such technology by coercive force. Finally, perceived data privacy risk was identified as a key driver in explaining user resistance to new eHealth technologies amongst physicians.

*Perceived coercive forces* The original research model hypothesized that when doctors feel increasingly pressured they would be driven to reduce their resistance to the 'eGK' technology. As a matter of fact the exact opposite seems to be the case. As doctors perceive coercive forces, they resist the 'eGK' technology irrespective of whether this pressure is enforced by the government or the general public. Such a reaction can be interpreted as an act of defiance. Indeed, in Germany doctors have repeatedly voiced their concerns in reaction to further advancements to rolling out the 'eGK' technology, for example at the Congresses for Physicians (Ärztetag) in 2007, 2008, 2009, 2010, 2012 and 2013. Similar findings were also observed in other national eHealth implementation projects, such as the NPfIT in the United Kingdom: "Coercive pressures to encourage regional hospitals to become more like teaching hospitals, and for IT literacy to increase among all health practitioners, tended to produce the opposite results insofar as these organizations reiterated their differences" (Currie 2012, p. 242).

*Perceived mimetic forces* Although the 'eGK' technology is still at an early stage of implementation, mimetic forces, i.e. the extent to which the industry, patients and even other doctors will perceive a user as the result of employing the technology, can reduce this user's resistance to the 'eGK' technology. A physician might therefore decide to resist less, either because she perceives that in the long run the technology will become an acknowledged standard amongst competitors or, moreover, because she believes that adopters of the technology will be more successful (Teo et al. 2003). Furthermore, at this stage of the implementation process the implications of the 'eGK' technology on doctors' ways of working remain somewhat unclear. Such uncertainty has in other cases shown to substantiate mimetic pressure (Currie 2012). This is also likely the case in the study of the 'eGK' technology.

*Perceived normative forces* The results show that perceived normative forces do not affect physicians' decision to resist the 'eGK' technology. As such, standards and norms set by the overall healthcare market have not gone so far as to influence doctors' decision to switch towards the 'eGK' technology. This might be explained by the fact that technological development is still in its early stage and doctors do not yet feel the need to comply with the wider social expectations, as also suggested in similar circumstanced by Jensen et al. (2009).

To further explore this argument, the same set of antecedents was used to test whether perceived normative forces would directly affect physicians' intention to use the 'eGK' technology. The construct for behavioral intention was therefore based on Venkatesh et al. (2003) (please also refer to Table 6.2 in Sect. 6.4).

The validity of this further model was ensured by using the same measurement criteria as in the main model where the construct of user resistance was the endogenous variable, as described above. All statistical measures hold and support the validity of the model (please refer to Table A.5 until Table A.8 in the Appendix).

Besides, using bootstrapping, the following effects could be deduced, as also depicted in Fig. 6.7: Two of the three perceived coercive forces, i.e. through the government and through the general public, previously measured as significantly affecting user resistance, no longer have a significant effect on behavioral intention. Instead, perceived normative forces from patients now load significantly on to the dependent variable ($\beta = +0.106$, $p < 0.05$). Again, perceived mimetic forces load significantly ($\beta = +0.172$, $p < 0.001$) and also have a positive effect on behavioral intention.

This phenomenon suggests that when perceiving top-down coercive forces, physicians resist new eHealth technologies. However, when a positive bottom-up demand for the technology is created, i.e. through mimetic force from peers or normative force from patients, physicians tend towards accepting the technology. The negative effect of perceived mimetic force on user resistance, measured above, further supports this line of reasoning.

*Perceived data privacy concerns* Most of the variance on user resistance was explained through the antecedent of perceived data privacy concerns. Such concerns were indeed repeatedly mentioned by many of the interview partners spoken to as part of the qualitative study in Phase II of this research. Perceived data privacy concerns have been widely discussed in the IS literature (Featherman and Pavlou 2003; Pavlou 2011; Smith et al. 2011; Xu et al. 2011). In the case of the 'eGK'

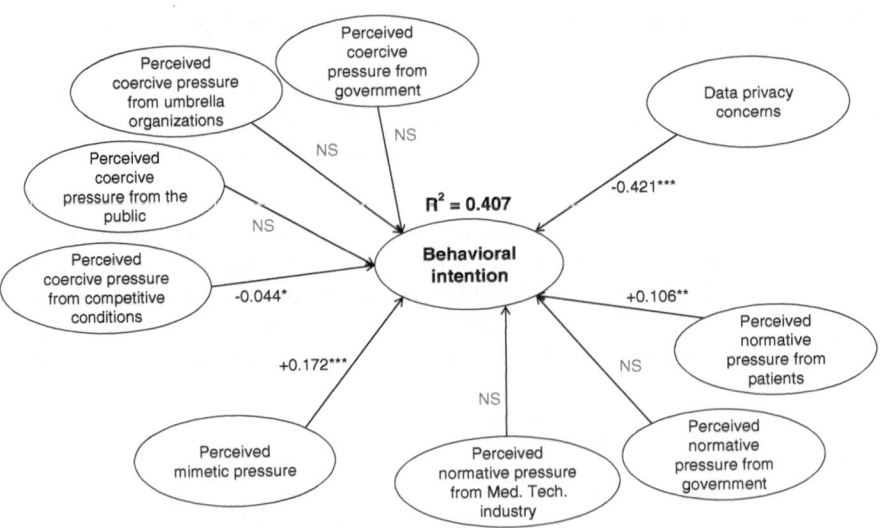

**Fig. 6.7** Results of hypothesis testing (comparative model). *Note *** $p < 0.01$; ** $p < 0.05$; * $p < 0.1$; NS* not significant at 0.1 level

technology, as with many eHealth technologies, such concerns appear particularly valid (Bansal et al. 2010). Finally, beyond what was actually measured in the model, doctors might not only be worried because they fear about their patient data but because they themselves are patients whenever they fall ill. Concerns of patients about the security of eHealth systems, such as the already commonly used 'Health Banks', are becoming increasingly relevant, too (Appari and Johnson 2010).

# Chapter 7
# Implications and Limitations of the Study

## 7.1 Theoretical Implications

This research aimed at theoretically developing and empirically testing a model that would better explain user resistance towards national eHealth systems. In a field yet relatively unexplored this thesis provides further scientific insights into the antecedents leading to user resistance towards eHealth technology implementation in particular and national information system implementations in general.

Much of the previous research on national eHealth implementations has been of a qualitative nature. The findings have, indeed, contributed rich theory to the field. This thesis on the 'eGK' technology, however, draws on both theoretical contributions within the field of information systems as well as variables brought to surface from exploratory qualitative data. It not only contributes towards this current academic agenda via a new theoretical model but also empirically validates this model. As such, this research has systematically identified a set of tangible variables around perceived societal forces which influence physicians' response to the introduction of new eHealth technology. Previous qualitative studies have suggested that such forces play a significant role in shaping large-scale eHealth implementation projects (Currie 2012; Jensen et al. 2009). The findings of the final quantitative study underline that perceived coercive and mimetic forces shape physicians' resistance behavior while perceived mimetic and normative forces can sway them towards intended use. Finally, the model also incorporates the contextually highly relevant factor of data privacy concerns.

The second major contribution is to the field of user resistance theory. While user resistance to information systems has been discussed by Markus (1983) as early as the 1980s, it has previously been ambiguously treated in relation to the more widely examined theories on user acceptance (Dwivedi et al. 2011). Nonetheless, recent studies have confirmed its unique theoretical contribution to the field as a separate phenomenon (Cenfetelli 2004; Lapointe and Beaudry 2014; van Offenbeek et al. 2013). Despite the recent increase in attention, very few studies

© Springer International Publishing Switzerland 2015
P. Klöcker, *Resistance Behavior to National eHealth Implementation Programs*,
Progress in IS, DOI 10.1007/978-3-319-17828-8_7

have empirically tested antecedents to user resistance. This study therefore provides a strong validation of user resistance theory. It extends Kim and Kankanhalli's (2009) as well as Eckhardt et al.'s (2009) research, who analyzed the influence of colleagues' respectively wider normative beliefs on adoption and non-adoption. Also, this study goes beyond previous research by systematically accounting for perceived societal forces, in the form of perceived coercive, mimetic and normative isomorphic forces, and by testing for their influence on user resistance.

It is important to notice, that while the theory around perceived isomorphic forces provided a suitable framework on which to base the final quantitative model, accounting for these forces according to the various stakeholders involved in the 'eGK' technology implementation process proved to be vital to the research. The so-called decomposition of the forces according to the various stakeholders was very much confirmed by the qualitative data obtained, whereby interview partners expressed individually perceived pressures from other stakeholders. The decomposition has furthermore proven to be particularly relevant in light of the fact that the findings on the effects of perceived coercive forces by the government and the public on user resistance run counter to what has previously been proposed by the relevant literature (Liang et al. 2007). At the same time, perceived coercive pressure from competitive forces was in line with previous suggestions.

In summary, this thesis answers other scholars' calls for further research on the often dispersed landscape of eHealth implementation (Currie 2012; Romanow et al. 2012). It develops and empirically tests a resistance model in this context with the aim of unveiling some of the motivations which drive physicians' behavior towards eHealth technology. This thesis will hopefully inspire further research surrounding the often complicated, costly and tiresome implementation of national eHealth infrastructures.

## 7.2 Practical Implications

On the practical side, this research provides an understanding of some of the difficulties implementers might be faced with when rolling out large-scale IS infrastructures, particularly in the healthcare sector. It therefore offers insights into which strategy governments might want to follow as they decide on implementing eHealth technologies. Indeed, they have to weigh up the option of following a rather coercive "push"-strategy, whereby they force the technology upon users, against a rather mimetic or normative "pull"-strategy, whereby they create demand from the physicians and patients alike. The findings suggest that coercive forces can be negatively perceived and continued pressure might in fact lead to increasingly adverse reactions and higher user resistance. Instead, governments might therefore want to follow a strategy whereby users start to build up a positive association with the new technology. Positively perceived mimetic force created amongst the doctors themselves as well as positively perceived normative force from patients will not only reduce resistance but may actually move doctors towards using eHealth systems.

## 7.3 Limitations of the Study and Suggestions for Further Research

Like all studies, this research, too, has some limitations which should be addressed by future studies. As a matter of fact, this research was conducted on the implementation of the 'eGK' technology in the German context. Germany has a very specific healthcare system involving certain stakeholders, such as the 'gematik' or the powerful umbrella organizations of payors and providers. Structures like these might not exist in other countries where eHealth projects may be implemented by different players and means. There, other stakeholders might drive physicians' behavior. Nonetheless, the perceived influence of some universally relevant players such as the government, the general public, patients and doctors were notably assessed. While the eHealth sector overall lends itself particularly well to observations of the effects of perceived societal forces on user resistance, given the strong influence of governmental and other regulatory bodies, further studies should be conducted in the context of other relevant nationwide IS programs. This will help to overcome possible limitations in terms of generalizability of the results.

Furthermore, looking at the 'eGK' implementation process from a longitudinal perspective might offer more insights into how physicians' resistance will change over time, especially once the 'eGK' technology is fully rolled out and used on a daily basis.

While the final set of variables for the quantitative study was deduced from the relevant literature and from succinct qualitative data, applying the lens of isomorphic forces, it should be acknowledged that other variables might affect user resistance to eHealth technology. Future research might therefore want to consider additional variables relevant to the area of study.

Finally, although the final quantitative study is based on a large overall sample of n = 469 physicians, the response rate to the questionnaire was just below 5 %. This might be considered relatively low in information systems related areas of research. Nonetheless, it should be noted that this research was conducted in a highly professional environment where data is known to be extremely difficult to obtain. Doctors often have very little time while being swamped with surveys and they are known to be concerned about the confidentiality of results (Kottke et al. 1990; VanGeest et al. 2007). Besides, as Flanigan et al. (2008) and Kellerman and Herold (2001) have shown nonresponse bias to be less of a concern for physician surveys.

Blair and Zinkhan (2006) furthermore support this notion. For them a representative sample is broad in terms of age and occupation as well as selected nonrandomly across diversified groups. According to the authors, such a sample is preferable even if it entails a lower response rate. Indeed, the study on the 'eGK' technology was carried out making use of a professional services firm that provided a representative list of physicians from across the country, by specialization, age and gender. Besides, the representativeness of the final sample was confirmed through a number of control variables, suggesting that the criteria by Blair and Zinkhan (2006) are arguably met.

Lastly and purely from a perspective of data analysis, the size of the sample was sufficient for running a statistically meaningful analysis considering the ten times rule of thumb as suggested by Barclay et al. (1995). In other words, the sample size is more than ten times larger than the largest number of structural paths pointed at the construct of user resistance.

# Chapter 8
# Conclusion

Conclusively, this thesis provides a multi-stage mixed method empirical approach, as it builds on relevant literature and an exploratory case study followed by theory development to test the final model in a large-scale, professionally conducted survey on German physicians' resistance to a new national eHealth system, namely the German 'eGK' technology.

In particular, a clear research gap surrounding individual physicians' resistance behavior towards new eHealth technologies was identified from a substantive, systematic literature review, which analyzed both the relevant literature on user resistance theory as well as on national eHealth implementation programs. The resulting concepts were subsequently tested in three phases each of which contribute extensively to the findings of the overall research:

Phase I tested for the applicability of user resistance theory, as previously developed in the field of information systems research, in the context of the 'eGK' technology. Making use of Kim and Kankanhalli's (2009) 'Status Quo Bias Model', individual user resistance was confirmed as a suitable dependent variable. However, none of the independent variables previously discussed in the literature proved to directly affect German physicians' resistance towards the 'eGK' technology.

In Phase II, therefore, a number of more suitable independent variables were identified from a wealth of qualitative data gathered both from exploratory qualitative data as well as semi-structured interviews with key stakeholders involved in the rollout process of the 'eGK' technology. This data suggested that societal forces, namely coercive, mimetic and normative isomorphic forces, as well as data privacy concerns heavily influence doctors' behavior towards the 'eGK' technology.

© Springer International Publishing Switzerland 2015
P. Klöcker, *Resistance Behavior to National eHealth Implementation Programs*,
Progress in IS, DOI 10.1007/978-3-319-17828-8_8

Finally, in Phase III, these newly identified antecedents were tested in a large-scale, professionally conducted survey amongst German physicians. The model was measured according to the current statistical criteria and found to meet the standard requirements as otherwise suggested in related studies in the field of information systems research. The results advocate that perceived coercive and mimetic societal forces as well as data privacy concerns significantly affect user resistance amongst physicians. Indeed, as physicians perceive coercive force from the government and the wider public they react adversely, further resisting the introduction of the 'eGK' technology. A second test was then performed to measure the effects of the same antecedents on physicians' behavioral intention to use the 'eGK' technology. By contrast, the results suggest that they might be swayed towards eHealth technology use if they perceive positive beliefs in the technology by either their patients or their peers.

This research, therefore, has meaningful implications for both theory and practice. It contributes to the literature on national eHealth implementation projects as well as user resistance theory in the field of information systems. Through its mixed method approach leveraging both qualitative and quantitative data it provides a particularly well-founded and complete analysis of the research question at hand. Finally, practical implications such as the potential importance of creating bottom-up demand for a new technology are discussed. Thus, this thesis provides a comprehensive, credible, and theoretically informed picture of physicians' resistance behavior towards national eHealth implementation projects.

# Appendix

## A.1 Cross Loadings of Items of the Pilot Study Sample

See Table A.1.

Table A.1 Cross loadings of items of the pilot study sample

| | Colleague opinion | Orga support for change | Perceived value | Resistance | Self-efficacy for change | Switching benefits | Switching costs |
|---|---|---|---|---|---|---|---|
| CGP 1 | **0.798** | 0.106 | 0.339 | −0.270 | 0.209 | 0.356 | −0.269 |
| CGP 2 | **0.843** | 0.424 | 0.280 | −0.292 | 0.298 | 0.366 | −0.398 |
| CGP 3 | **0.868** | 0.261 | 0.355 | −0.385 | 0.261 | 0.465 | −0.543 |
| OGS 2 | 0.238 | **0.938** | 0.119 | −0.239 | 0.369 | 0.141 | −0.298 |
| OGS 3 | 0.324 | **0.867** | 0.162 | −0.246 | 0.224 | 0.136 | −0.199 |
| OGS 4 | 0.209 | **0.463** | 0.023 | 0.019 | 0.210 | 0.128 | −0.243 |
| PVL 1 | 0.334 | 0.077 | **0.886** | −0.503 | 0.123 | 0.783 | −0.592 |
| PVL 2 | 0.386 | 0.094 | **0.952** | −0.507 | 0.074 | 0.765 | −0.522 |
| PVL 3 | 0.344 | 0.225 | **0.901** | −0.448 | 0.150 | 0.663 | −0.538 |
| RTC 1 | −0.368 | −0.160 | −0.534 | **0.930** | −0.188 | −0.544 | 0.578 |
| RTC 2 | −0.310 | −0.344 | −0.405 | **0.912** | −0.243 | −0.491 | 0.579 |
| RTC 3 | −0.402 | −0.111 | −0.553 | **0.834** | −0.204 | −0.588 | 0.546 |
| RTC 5 | −0.292 | −0.213 | −0.402 | **0.896** | −0.188 | −0.446 | 0.510 |
| SFC 1 | 0.253 | 0.288 | 0.130 | −0.205 | **0.925** | 0.170 | −0.504 |
| SFC 2 | 0.069 | 0.281 | −0.009 | −0.118 | **0.888** | 0.084 | −0.355 |
| SFC 3 | 0.421 | 0.359 | 0.170 | −0.263 | **0.883** | 0.266 | −0.562 |
| SWB 1 | 0.413 | 0.125 | 0.729 | −0.580 | 0.254 | **0.913** | −0.650 |
| SWB 2 | 0.470 | 0.164 | 0.783 | −0.534 | 0.192 | **0.949** | −0.630 |
| SWB 3 | 0.475 | 0.150 | 0.738 | −0.505 | 0.168 | **0.956** | −0.601 |

(continued)

© Springer International Publishing Switzerland 2015
P. Klöcker, *Resistance Behavior to National eHealth Implementation Programs*,
Progress in IS, DOI 10.1007/978-3-319-17828-8

**Table A.1** (continued)

| | Colleague opinion | Orga support for change | Perceived value | Resistance | Self-efficacy for change | Switching benefits | Switching costs |
|---|---|---|---|---|---|---|---|
| **SWB 4** | 0.448 | 0.188 | 0.794 | −0.569 | 0.175 | **0.939** | −0.681 |
| **SWC 1** | −0.019 | 0.027 | −0.101 | 0.091 | −0.236 | −0.097 | **0.300** |
| **SWC 2** | −0.414 | −0.273 | −0.550 | 0.623 | −0.507 | −0.572 | **0.870** |
| **SWC 3** | −0.531 | −0.306 | −0.556 | 0.519 | −0.375 | −0.664 | **0.816** |
| **SWC 4** | −0.309 | −0.202 | −0.377 | 0.379 | −0.455 | −0.451 | **0.781** |

## A.2 Interview Partners in Semi-structured Interviews

See Table A.2.

**Table A.2** Interview partners for qualitative study

| Stakeholder group | Position | Type of interview |
|---|---|---|
| Government | Government official, responsible for telematics-related functions and 'eGK' technology implementation project | Semi-structured interview |
| 'gematik' | Direct consultant to 'gematik'; working on technical specifications as well as several sub-projects, i.e. field-test rollout process | |
| Payor organizations | Representative from payor umbrella organization; working on telematics-related functions, focus on 'eGK' technology implementation project | |
| | Three representatives from large public insurance company; specialist on telematics-related functions and 'eGK' technology implementation project (same interview) | |
| | Representative from large public insurance company; specialist on telematics-related functions and 'eGK' technology implementation project | |
| | Representative from large private insurance company; specialist on telematics-related functions and 'eGK' technology implementation project | |
| Provider organizations | Representative from provider umbrella organization; working on telematics-related functions, focus on 'eGK' technology implementation project | |
| | Five individual doctors (separate interviews) | |
| Medical technology provider | Manager of large health connectivity provider; involved in 'eGK' technology implementation project | |
| External consultant | Senior management consultant; worked on several sub-projects to introduce 'eGK' technology | |

## A.3 Means and Standard Deviations at Construct Level of Main Model

See Table A.3.

**Table A.3** Means and standard deviations at construct level (main model)

| Construct | Mean | Standard deviation |
|---|---|---|
| Resistance | 4.960 | 2.036 |
| Coercive pressure government | 5.645 | 1.607 |
| Coercive pressure umbrella organizations | 5.762 | 1.590 |
| Coercive pressure public opinion | 3.273 | 1.927 |
| Coercive competitive conditions | 2.678 | 1.835 |
| Mimetic pressure | 2.550 | 1.465 |
| Normative pressure Med Tech industry | 5.607 | 1.625 |
| Normative pressure patients | 1.993 | 1.231 |
| Normative pressure government | 6.022 | 1.307 |
| Data privacy concerns | 5.945 | 1.461 |

## A.4 Set of Socio-demographic Variables and Control Variables in Main Model

See Table A.4.

**Table A.4** Set of socio-demographic variables and control variables (main model)

| Variable | Item | Scaling |
|---|---|---|
| Occupation | Ihr Beruf | (1) Ärztin/Arzt<br>(2) Med. Fachangestellte(r) |
| Specialization | Die Fachrichtung/en Ihrer Praxis (Mehrfachnennung möglich) | (1) Allgemeinmediziner<br>(2) Augenheilkunde<br>(3) Dermatologie (Haut- und Geschlechtskrankheiten)<br>(4) Diagnostische Radiologie<br>(5) Frauenheilkunde und Geburtshilfe<br>(6) Hals-Nasen-Ohrenheilkunde<br>(7) Innere Medizin<br>(8) Kinder- und Jugendlichenpsychotherapeut |

(continued)

**Table A.4** (continued)

| Variable | Item | Scaling |
|----------|------|---------|
| | | (9) Kinderheilkunde / Kinder- und Jugendmedizin<br>(10) Neurologie<br>(11) Orthopädie<br>(12) Orthopädie und Unfallchirurgie<br>(13) Praktischer Arzt (ohne FA Allgemeinmedizin)<br>(14) Psychiatrie und Psychotherapie<br>(15) Psychologischer Psychotherapeut<br>(16) Psychosomatische Medizin und Psychotherapie<br>(17) Urologie<br>(18) Sonstige Fachrichtung: |
| KV-SafeNet | Benutzen Sie bereits Online-Anwendungen im Rahmen von KV-SafeNet? | (1) Ja<br>(2) Nein<br>(3) Kenne ich nicht |
| Age | Ihr Alter | (1) Unter 30 Jahren<br>(2) 30-44 Jahre<br>(3) 45-59 Jahre<br>(4) 60 und älter |
| Gender | Sind Sie? | (1) Männlich<br>(2) Weiblich |
| Type of medical practice | In welcher Praxisform sind Sie tätig? | (1) Einzelpraxis<br>(2) Praxisgemeinschaft<br>(3) BAG<br>(4) ÜBAG<br>(5) MVZ |
| Internet | Nutzen Sie das Internet an Ihrem Praxisrechner? | (1) Ja<br>(2) Nein |

# A.5 Loadings of Comparative Model

See Table A.5.

**Table A.5** Item means and standard deviations, outer loadings and their statistical significance (comparative model)

| Item | Mean | Standard deviation | Outer loading | T Statistics (|O/STERR|) |
|---|---|---|---|---|
| BI 1 | 2.154 | 2.173 | 0.973 | 216.414 |
| BI 3 | 2.501 | 2.163 | 0.960 | 142.940 |
| BI 4 | 2.458 | 2.114 | 0.954 | 93.222 |
| BI 5 | 2.829 | 2.236 | 0.898 | 59.977 |
| CP1a | 5.454 | 1.869 | 0.764 | 15.325 |
| CP1c | 5.729 | 1.879 | 0.906 | 48.774 |
| CP1e | 5.751 | 1.762 | 0.922 | 81.824 |
| CP2a | 5.770 | 1.760 | 0.872 | 37.542 |
| CP2b | 5.765 | 1.812 | 0.918 | 72.591 |
| CP2c | 5.840 | 1.681 | 0.906 | 68.231 |
| CP2d | 5.672 | 1.788 | 0.912 | 72.130 |
| CP3b | 3.045 | 2.099 | 0.848 | 4.269 |
| CP3c | 3.328 | 2.148 | 0.804 | 3.710 |
| CP3d | 3.446 | 2.101 | 0.977 | 4.233 |
| CP4a | 2.582 | 1.988 | 0.928 | 71.769 |
| CP4b | 2.725 | 2.071 | 0.840 | 26.536 |
| CP4d | 2.810 | 2.097 | 0.907 | 58.803 |
| CP4e | 2.595 | 1.951 | 0.922 | 55.176 |
| MP1 | 2.761 | 1.760 | 0.889 | 56.573 |
| MP3 | 2.392 | 1.531 | 0.854 | 42.202 |
| MP7 | 2.497 | 1.737 | 0.870 | 41.321 |
| NOP1a | 5.655 | 1.681 | 0.964 | 6.765 |
| NOP1b | 5.588 | 1.689 | 0.962 | 6.445 |
| NOP1c | 5.578 | 1.730 | 0.927 | 5.996 |
| NOP2a | 2.143 | 1.458 | 0.888 | 46.478 |
| NOP2b | 1.857 | 1.256 | 0.897 | 43.565 |
| NOP2c | 2.006 | 1.398 | 0.905 | 56.695 |
| NOP2d | 1.964 | 1.367 | 0.901 | 43.118 |
| NOP3a | 6.009 | 1.384 | 0.946 | 26.554 |
| NOP3b | 6.021 | 1.360 | 0.940 | 22.542 |
| NOP3d | 6.036 | 1.416 | 0.934 | 24.899 |
| PDSR1 | 6.151 | 1.675 | 0.875 | 52.231 |
| PDSR2 | 6.019 | 1.592 | 0.795 | 24.830 |
| PDSR4 | 5.959 | 1.762 | 0.840 | 30.138 |
| PPR1 | 5.804 | 1.863 | 0.871 | 46.013 |
| PPR2 | 5.789 | 1.849 | 0.788 | 26.153 |

## A.6 Cronbach Alphas, Composite Reliabilities and AVEs of Comparative Model

See Table A.6.

**Table A.6** Cronbach Alphas, composite reliabilities and AVEs (comparative model)

| Construct | Cronbach Alpha | Composite reliabilities | AVE |
|---|---|---|---|
| Age | 1 | 1 | 1 |
| Coercive pressure comp. conditions | 0.927 | 0.944 | 0.810 |
| Coercive pressure government | 0.846 | 0.901 | 0.751 |
| Coercive pressure public opinion | 0.896 | 0.910 | 0.773 |
| Coercive pressure umbrella org. | 0.924 | 0.946 | 0.814 |
| Data privacy concerns | 0.891 | 0.920 | 0.696 |
| Intention | 0.961 | 0.972 | 0.896 |
| Internet | 1 | 1 | 1 |
| KV-SafeNet | 1 | 1 | 1 |
| Mimetic pressure | 0.842 | 0.904 | 0.759 |
| Normative pressure government | 0.936 | 0.958 | 0.884 |
| Normative pressure Med-Tech. industry | 0.952 | 0.966 | 0.905 |
| Normative pressure patients | 0.920 | 0.943 | 0.806 |
| Size of practice | 1 | 1 | 1 |

*Note* Age, Internet, KV-SafeNet and Size of Practice are control variables

## A.7 Square Root of AVEs and Correlations of Comparative Model

See Table A.7.

## A.8 Cross Loadings of Items in the Sample of Comparative Model

See Table A.8.

**Table A.7** Square root of AVEs and correlations (comparative model)

| Construct | 1 | 2 | 3 | 4 | 5 | 6 | 7 | 8 | 9 | 10 | 11 | 12 | 13 | 14 |
|---|---|---|---|---|---|---|---|---|---|---|---|---|---|---|
| Age | **1.000** | – | – | – | – | – | – | – | – | – | – | – | – | – |
| CP Comp. Conditions | 0.037 | **0.900** | – | – | – | – | – | – | – | – | – | – | – | – |
| CP Govt. | 0.053 | 0.003 | **0.867** | – | – | – | – | – | – | – | – | – | – | – |
| CP Public opinion | 0.078 | 0.300 | 0.262 | **0.879** | – | – | – | – | – | – | – | – | – | – |
| CP Umbrella Org. | 0.071 | 0.018 | 0.696 | 0.343 | **0.902** | – | – | – | – | – | – | – | – | – |
| Data privacy | 0.018 | −0.171 | 0.444 | 0.223 | 0.474 | **0.834** | – | – | – | – | – | – | – | – |
| Behavioral Intention | 0.018 | 0.280 | −0.324 | −0.107 | −0.321 | −0.558 | **0.947** | – | – | – | – | – | – | – |
| Internet | −0.040 | −0.156 | 0.128 | 0.097 | 0.178 | 0.223 | −0.237 | **1.000** | – | – | – | – | – | – |
| KV-SafeNet | −0.049 | −0.163 | 0.112 | 0.058 | 0.131 | 0.068 | −0.164 | 0.204 | **1.000** | – | – | – | – | – |
| MP | −0.032 | 0.570 | −0.209 | 0.167 | −0.234 | −0.260 | 0.394 | −0.209 | −0.171 | **0.871** | – | – | – | – |
| NP Govt. | 0.055 | 0.057 | 0.444 | 0.170 | 0.323 | 0.144 | −0.137 | 0.044 | 0.123 | −0.017 | **0.940** | – | – | – |
| NP Med-Tech | 0.090 | 0.077 | 0.157 | 0.171 | 0.145 | 0.126 | −0.047 | −0.065 | 0.042 | 0.089 | 0.357 | **0.951** | – | – |
| NP Patients | −0.002 | 0.266 | −0.271 | 0.073 | −0.258 | −0.327 | 0.365 | −0.179 | −0.070 | 0.491 | −0.031 | 0.058 | **0.898** | – |
| Size of practice | −0.134 | −0.046 | 0.007 | −0.020 | −0.068 | −0.071 | 0.055 | −0.138 | −0.061 | −0.025 | 0.022 | 0.077 | −0.003 | **1.000** |

*Note* Square root of AVEs displayed on diagonal; *CP* = coercive pressure; *MP* = mimetic pressure; *NP* = normative pressure

**Table A.8** Cross loadings of items in the sample (comparative model)

| | Age | CP Comp. Conditions | CP Govt | CP Public opinion | CP Umbrella Org. | Data privacy | Intention | Internet | KV-SafeNet | MP | NOP Govt | NP MedTech | NP Patients | Size of practice |
|---|---|---|---|---|---|---|---|---|---|---|---|---|---|---|
| Age | **1.000** | 0.037 | 0.053 | 0.078 | 0.071 | 0.018 | 0.018 | -0.040 | -0.049 | -0.032 | 0.055 | 0.090 | -0.002 | -0.134 |
| BI 1 | 0.018 | 0.257 | -0.306 | -0.113 | -0.307 | -0.531 | **0.973** | -0.211 | -0.142 | 0.370 | -0.135 | -0.045 | 0.346 | 0.031 |
| BI 3 | 0.029 | 0.258 | -0.290 | -0.082 | -0.284 | -0.529 | **0.960** | -0.214 | -0.125 | 0.354 | -0.129 | -0.043 | 0.348 | 0.028 |
| BI 4 | 0.003 | 0.257 | -0.294 | -0.088 | -0.285 | -0.511 | **0.954** | -0.214 | -0.142 | 0.362 | -0.091 | -0.040 | 0.346 | 0.040 |
| BI 5 | 0.019 | 0.286 | -0.332 | -0.118 | -0.335 | -0.537 | **0.898** | -0.253 | -0.208 | 0.401 | -0.161 | -0.051 | 0.342 | 0.106 |
| CP 1a | 0.036 | 0.114 | **0.764** | 0.167 | 0.514 | 0.237 | -0.125 | 0.077 | 0.100 | -0.079 | 0.370 | 0.076 | -0.141 | -0.026 |
| CP 1c | 0.071 | 0.028 | **0.906** | 0.286 | 0.672 | 0.453 | -0.294 | 0.133 | 0.052 | -0.169 | 0.370 | 0.137 | -0.243 | -0.003 |
| CP 1e | 0.031 | -0.060 | **0.922** | 0.211 | 0.613 | 0.402 | -0.342 | 0.111 | 0.139 | -0.239 | 0.426 | 0.166 | -0.276 | 0.026 |
| CP 2a | 0.061 | 0.040 | 0.618 | 0.246 | **0.872** | 0.342 | -0.242 | 0.121 | 0.137 | -0.190 | 0.342 | 0.111 | -0.206 | -0.061 |
| CP 2b | 0.053 | 0.035 | 0.677 | 0.343 | **0.918** | 0.447 | -0.298 | 0.172 | 0.094 | -0.206 | 0.284 | 0.158 | -0.225 | -0.031 |
| CP 2c | 0.062 | -0.028 | 0.617 | 0.315 | **0.906** | 0.439 | -0.295 | 0.162 | 0.149 | -0.237 | 0.306 | 0.142 | -0.255 | -0.088 |
| CP 2d | 0.080 | 0.022 | 0.604 | 0.322 | **0.912** | 0.466 | -0.314 | 0.181 | 0.100 | -0.211 | 0.248 | 0.109 | -0.241 | -0.065 |
| CP 3b | 0.071 | 0.327 | 0.189 | **0.848** | 0.252 | 0.159 | -0.042 | 0.039 | 0.000 | 0.200 | 0.113 | 0.135 | 0.105 | -0.016 |
| CP 3c | 0.047 | 0.308 | 0.248 | **0.804** | 0.302 | 0.162 | -0.016 | 0.058 | 0.032 | 0.191 | 0.161 | 0.154 | 0.117 | -0.047 |
| CP 3d | 0.077 | 0.261 | 0.261 | **0.977** | 0.344 | 0.230 | -0.129 | 0.112 | 0.074 | 0.136 | 0.173 | 0.168 | 0.050 | -0.016 |
| CP 4a | 0.036 | **0.928** | 0.045 | 0.296 | 0.077 | -0.111 | 0.227 | -0.153 | -0.138 | 0.518 | 0.057 | 0.083 | 0.217 | -0.056 |
| CP 4b | 0.120 | **0.840** | 0.116 | 0.445 | 0.150 | -0.018 | 0.134 | -0.065 | -0.080 | 0.424 | 0.056 | 0.114 | 0.174 | -0.084 |
| CP 4d | -0.012 | **0.907** | -0.104 | 0.150 | -0.123 | -0.277 | 0.349 | -0.173 | -0.192 | 0.573 | 0.056 | 0.054 | 0.303 | -0.010 |
| CP 4e | 0.053 | **0.922** | 0.064 | 0.343 | 0.103 | -0.084 | 0.196 | -0.121 | -0.125 | 0.478 | 0.036 | 0.051 | 0.201 | -0.053 |
| Internet | -0.040 | -0.156 | 0.128 | 0.097 | 0.178 | 0.223 | -0.237 | **1.000** | 0.204 | -0.209 | 0.044 | -0.065 | -0.179 | -0.138 |
| KV SafeNet | -0.049 | -0.163 | 0.112 | 0.058 | 0.131 | 0.068 | -0.164 | 0.204 | **1.000** | -0.171 | 0.123 | 0.042 | -0.070 | -0.061 |

(continued)

Table A.8 (continued)

| | Age | CP Comp. Conditions | CP Govt | CP Public opinion | CP Umbrella Org. | Data privacy | Intention | Internet | KV-SafeNet | MP | NOP Govt | NP MedTech | NP Patients | Size of practice |
|---|---|---|---|---|---|---|---|---|---|---|---|---|---|---|
| MP 1 | -0.022 | 0.479 | -0.167 | 0.130 | -0.193 | -0.212 | 0.334 | -0.142 | -0.157 | **0.889** | 0.010 | 0.094 | 0.368 | -0.038 |
| MP 3 | -0.031 | 0.414 | -0.217 | 0.119 | -0.259 | -0.271 | 0.366 | -0.194 | -0.125 | **0.854** | -0.052 | 0.040 | 0.519 | -0.024 |
| MP 7 | -0.031 | 0.607 | -0.157 | 0.190 | -0.154 | -0.191 | 0.326 | -0.208 | -0.167 | **0.870** | 0.000 | 0.102 | 0.385 | -0.002 |
| NOP 1a | 0.088 | 0.072 | 0.131 | 0.176 | 0.134 | 0.132 | -0.050 | -0.075 | 0.031 | 0.083 | 0.301 | **0.964** | 0.038 | 0.076 |
| NOP 1b | 0.093 | 0.068 | 0.185 | 0.159 | 0.156 | 0.122 | -0.051 | -0.052 | 0.047 | 0.076 | 0.380 | **0.962** | 0.066 | 0.079 |
| NOP 1c | 0.061 | 0.098 | 0.102 | 0.139 | 0.097 | 0.083 | -0.016 | -0.059 | 0.049 | 0.119 | 0.348 | **0.927** | 0.075 | 0.052 |
| NOP 2a | 0.029 | 0.219 | -0.264 | 0.012 | -0.250 | -0.308 | 0.348 | -0.172 | -0.055 | 0.413 | -0.026 | 0.049 | **0.888** | 0.011 |
| NOP 2b | -0.021 | 0.258 | -0.256 | 0.117 | -0.232 | -0.306 | 0.313 | -0.150 | -0.053 | 0.444 | -0.039 | 0.054 | **0.897** | -0.013 |
| NOP 2c | -0.016 | 0.259 | -0.205 | 0.098 | -0.230 | -0.272 | 0.316 | -0.152 | -0.074 | 0.457 | 0.014 | 0.059 | **0.905** | -0.011 |
| NOP 2d | -0.002 | 0.220 | -0.244 | 0.043 | -0.215 | -0.289 | 0.332 | -0.166 | -0.068 | 0.450 | -0.059 | 0.046 | **0.901** | 0.000 |
| NOP 3a | 0.032 | 0.050 | 0.414 | 0.168 | 0.318 | 0.131 | -0.127 | 0.048 | 0.115 | -0.012 | **0.946** | 0.333 | -0.010 | 0.030 |
| NOP 3b | 0.075 | 0.057 | 0.438 | 0.153 | 0.303 | 0.145 | -0.154 | 0.042 | 0.120 | -0.029 | **0.940** | 0.355 | -0.044 | 0.007 |
| NOP 3d | 0.038 | 0.054 | 0.387 | 0.161 | 0.286 | 0.125 | -0.091 | 0.033 | 0.109 | -0.002 | **0.934** | 0.307 | -0.030 | 0.029 |
| PDSR 1 | 0.000 | -0.181 | 0.326 | 0.188 | 0.358 | **0.875** | -0.531 | 0.176 | 0.016 | -0.242 | 0.097 | 0.117 | -0.300 | -0.078 |
| PDSR 2 | 0.045 | -0.147 | 0.345 | 0.165 | 0.349 | **0.795** | -0.394 | 0.201 | 0.096 | -0.175 | 0.150 | 0.148 | -0.217 | -0.048 |
| PDSR 4 | 0.028 | -0.170 | 0.330 | 0.147 | 0.396 | **0.840** | -0.479 | 0.203 | 0.016 | -0.271 | 0.103 | 0.103 | -0.307 | -0.037 |
| PPR 1 | -0.029 | -0.125 | 0.429 | 0.221 | 0.445 | **0.871** | -0.482 | 0.169 | 0.104 | -0.206 | 0.134 | 0.099 | -0.273 | -0.094 |
| PPR 2 | 0.041 | -0.083 | 0.435 | 0.211 | 0.436 | **0.788** | -0.424 | 0.188 | 0.066 | -0.179 | 0.128 | 0.062 | -0.258 | -0.031 |
| Practice | -0.134 | -0.046 | 0.007 | -0.020 | -0.068 | -0.071 | 0.055 | -0.138 | -0.061 | -0.025 | 0.022 | 0.077 | -0.003 | **1.000** |

# A.9 Introduction to Questionnaire

See Fig. A.9.

Sehr geehrte Damen und Herren,

im Namen des **Lehrstuhls für Information Systems & Management, Prof. Dr. Daniel Veit,** der Universität Augsburg laden wir Sie herzlich ein, an einer **Umfrage zur 'Elektronischen Gesundheitskarte' ('eGK')** teilzunehmen.

Mit der Einführung der 'eGK' will der Gesetzgeber erreichen, dass Sie im Behandlungsablauf wichtige medizinische Informationen mit Ihren Kollegen/Kolleginnen auf elektronischem Wege austauschen können. Die sichere Online-Anbindung der Praxis gemäß Gesetz SGB-V soll durch die Telematikinfrastruktur ermöglicht werden. Diese verbindet zukünftig die IT-Systeme aus Arztpraxen, Apotheken und Krankenhäusern miteinander.

Die Einführung der 'eGK' hat der Lehrstuhl zum Anlass genommen, ein wissenschaftliches Forschungsvorhaben zur Messung der Akzeptanz der neuen Technologie zu initiieren.

Der dreiteilige Fragebogen ist der zentrale Bestandteil des Forschungsvorhabens und auch eines darauf aufbauenden Promotionsvorhabens. Daher würden wir uns freuen, wenn Sie sich **ca. 15 Minuten** Zeit nähmen, alle Fragen entsprechend zu beantworten. Selbstverständlich werden Ihre **Antworten streng vertraulich und anonymisiert behandelt.**

Wir bitten Sie, den ausgefüllten **Fragebogen bis zum 28.02.2014 abzusenden.** Sollten Sie an den Ergebnissen unserer Studie interessiert sein, haben Sie die Möglichkeit, am Ende des Fragebogens Ihre E-Mail-Adresse über eine separate Funktion zu verschicken. Somit ist sichergestellt, dass diese E-Mail-Adresse Ihren Antworten im Rahmen des Fragebogens nicht zugeordnet werden kann. Wir werden Ihnen die Ergebnisse der Studie dann zu gegebenen Zeitpunkt an diese E-Mail-Adresse zusenden.

Sollten Sie weitere Fragen haben, stehen wir Ihnen jederzeit gerne unter kloecken@is-augsburg.de zur Verfügung.

Vielen Dank für Ihre Teilnahme!

MSc. Philipp Klöcker                        Prof. Dr. Daniel Veit

>>> Start Umfrage <<<

MSc. Philipp Klöcker, Doktorand
University of Augsburg, School of Business and Economics
Chair of Information Systems & Management, Prof. Dr. Daniel Veit
Room J 1410, Universitätsstraße 16, 86159 Augsburg
Tel.: +49 (0)160 96201111, Fax: +49 (0) 821 598-4432
E-Mail: kloecker@is-augsburg.de
www.wiwi.uni-augsburg.de/de/bwl/veit

**Fig. A.9** Introduction to final questionnaire

# A.10 Explanatory Text to Questionnaire

See Fig. A.10.

### Teil 1 - Ausgangsszenario:

Unser Lehrstuhl hat die Einführung der ‚Elektronischen Gesundheitskarte' (‚eGK') zum Anlass genommen, zu untersuchen, warum Nutzer eine neue Technologie akzeptieren oder ihr ggf. kritisch gegenüber stehen. Letzteres geschieht häufig vor dem Hintergrund, dass sich tägliche Arbeitsabläufe durch den Einsatz der neuen Technologie verändern. So, nehmen wir an, werden auch Sie als Ärztin/Arzt oder Medizinische(r) Fachangestellte(r) durch den Einsatz der 'eGK' zukünftig Veränderungen in Ihrer Arbeitsweise erfahren.

Zum Beispiel: Beim Besuch des Patienten in der Arztpraxis wird die 'eGK' gesteckt. Die Versichertenstammdaten (VSDM) des Patienten werden automatisch bei der zuständigen Krankenkasse abgefragt. Die Gültigkeit der Karte sowie die Aktualität der Stammdaten werden überprüft. Als gestohlen gemeldete Karten können ebenfalls identifiziert werden. Auch bei der Anwendung von medizinischen Funktionalitäten, wie z.B. das Pflegen einer elektronischen Patientenakte, kommt die Telematikinfrastruktur zum Einsatz. Zugleich erfordern diese Funktionen die Verwendung bzw. die Authentifizierung Ihrerseits durch den

Heilberufsausweis (HBA).

Vor diesem Hintergrund fragen die folgenden Aussagen **Ihre persönliche Einstellung zur ‚eGK'** ab.
Bitte kreuzen Sie an, inwiefern Sie den folgenden Aussagen zustimmen.

**Fig. A.10** Explanatory text to questionnaire

# References

Aanestad, M., & Jensen, T. B. (2011). Building nation-wide information infrastructures in healthcare through modular implementation strategies. *The Journal of Strategic Information Systems, 20*(2), 161–176.

Agarwal, R., Gao, G. (Gordon), DesRoches, C., & Jha, A. K. (2010, November). Research commentary—the digital transformation of healthcare: Current status and the road ahead. *Information Systems Research, 21*(4), 796–809.

Ajzen, I. (1985). From intentions to actions: A theory of planned behavior. In P. D. J. Kuhl & D. J. Beckmann (Eds.), *Action control* (pp. 11–39). Berlin Heidelberg: Springer.

Albers, S. (2010). PLS and success factor studies in marketing. In: V. Esposito Vinzi, W. W. Chin, J. Henseler & H. Wang (Eds.), *Handbook of partial least squares*. Berlin, Heidelberg: Springer.

Anderson, C. L., & Agarwal, R. (2011, April). The digitization of healthcare: boundary risks, emotion, and consumer willingness to disclose personal health information. *Information Systems Research, 22*(3), 469–490.

Appari, A., & Johnson, M. E. (2010). Information security and privacy in healthcare: Current state of research. *International Journal of Internet and Enterprise Management, 6*(4), 279–314.

Ash, J. S., & Bates, D. W. (2005). Factors and forces affecting EHR system adoption: Report of a 2004 ACMI discussion. *Journal of the American Medical Informatics Association : JAMIA, 12*(1), 8–11.

Avison, D., & Young, T. (2007). Time to rethink health care and ICT? *Communications of the ACM, 50*(6), 69–74.

Azad, B., & King, N. (2008, July). Enacting computer workaround practices within a medication dispensing system. *European Journal of Information Systems, 17*(3), 264–278.

Azad, B., & King, N. (2012, July). Institutionalized computer workaround practices in a Mediterranean country: An examination of two organizations. *European Journal of Information Systems, 21*(4), 358–372.

Babin, B. J., Hair, J. F., & Boles, J. S. (2008, September). Publishing research in marketing journals using structural equation modeling. *The Journal of Marketing Theory and Practice, 16*(4), 279–286.

Backhaus, K., Erichson, B., Plinke, W., & Weiber, R. (2010). Multivariate Analysemethoden: Eine anwendungsorientierte Einführung, Auflage: 13., überarb. Aufl. 2011., Berlin u.a.: Springer.

Bagozzi, R. P. (1980). *Causal models in marketing*. New York: Wiley.

Bagozzi, R., & Phillips, L. (1982). Representing and testing organizational theories: a holistic construal. *Administrative Science Quarterly, 27*(3), 459–489.

Bandura, A. (1997). *Self-efficacy in changing societies*. Cambridge: Cambridge University Press.

Bansal, G., Zahedi, F. M., & Gefen, D. (2010, May). The impact of personal dispositions on information sensitivity, privacy concern and trust in disclosing health information online. *Decision Support Systems, 49*(2), 138–150.

© Springer International Publishing Switzerland 2015
P. Klöcker, *Resistance Behavior to National eHealth Implementation Programs*, Progress in IS, DOI 10.1007/978-3-319-17828-8

Barclay, D., Higgins, C., & Thompson, R. (1995). The partial least squares (PLS) approach to causal modeling: Personal computer adoption and use as an illustration. *Technology Studies, 2*(2), 285–309.

Barth, M., & Veit, D. (2011). Which processes do users not want online? extending process virtualization theory. In: *Proceedings of the International Conference on Information Systems 2011*, Shanghai, China.

Becerra-Fernandez, I., & Sabherwal, R. (2001, May). Organizational knowledge management: A contingency perspective. *Journal of Management Information System, 18*(1), 23–55.

Berner, E. S., Detmer, D. E., & Simborg, D. (2005). Will the wave finally break? a brief view of the adoption of electronic medical records in the united states. *Journal of the American Medical Informatics Association : JAMIA, 12*(1), 3–7.

Bhattacherjee, A., & Hikmet, N. (2007). Physicians' resistance toward healthcare information technology: A theoretical model and empirical test. *European Journal of Information Systems, 16*(6), 725–737.

Bhattacherjee, A., & Premkumar, G. (2004, June). Understanding changes in belief and attitude toward information technology usage: A theoretical model and longitudinal test. *MIS Quarterly, 28*(2), 229–254.

Blair, E., & Zinkhan, G. M. (2006). Nonresponse and generalizability in academic research. *Journal of the Academy of Marketing Science, 34*(1), 4–7.

Bollen, K. A. (1989). *Structural equations with latent variables.* Chapel Hill, USA: Wiley.

Brennan, S. (2007, July). The biggest computer programme in the world ever! How's it going? *Journal of Information Technology, 22*(3), 202–211.

Brown, S. A., & Venkatesh, V. (2005, September). Model of adoption of technology in households: A baseline model test and extension incorporating household life cycle. *MIS Quarterly, 29*(3), 399–426.

Burnkrant, R. E., & Cousineau, A. (1975). Informational and normative social influence in buyer behavior. *Journal of Consumer Research, 2*(3), 206–215.

Cao, J., Crews, J. M., Lin, M., Deokar, A., Burgoon, J. K., & Nunamaker, J. F. (2006, April). Interactions between system evaluation and theory testing: A demonstration of the power of a mulitfaceted approach to systems research. *Journal of Management Information Systems, 22*(4), 207–235.

Cassel, C., Hackl, P., & Westlund, A. H. (1999). Robustness of partial least-squares method for estimating latent variable quality structures. *Journal of Applied Statistics, 26*(4), 435–446.

Cenfetelli, R. T. (2004). Inhibitors and enablers as dual factor concepts in technology usage. *Journal of the Association for Information Systems, 5*(11), 472–492.

Cenfetelli, R. T., & Bassellier, G. (2009). Interpretation of formative measurement in information systems research. *MIS Quarterly, 33*(4), 689–707.

Chen, H. (2013). *Effects of institutional pressure and dynamic capabilities on operational performance of US long-term healthcare providers.* Arlington: University of Texas at Arlington

Chiasson, M. W., & Davidson, E. (2004, July). Pushing the contextual envelope: Developing and diffusing IS theory for health information systems research. *Information and Organization, 14*(3), 155–188.

Chin, W. W. (1998). Commentary: Issues and opinion on structural equation modeling. *MIS Quarterly, 22*(1), vii–xvi.

Chin, W. W. (2010). How to write up and report PLS analyses. In V. E. Vinzi, W. W. Chin, J. Henseler, & H. Wang (Eds.), *Handbook of partial least squares* (pp. 655–690). Berlin Heidelberg: Springer.

Churchill, G. A. (1979). A paradigm for developing better measures of marketing constructs. *Journal of Marketing Research, 16*(1), 64–73.

Clegg, C., & Shepherd, C. (2007, July). 'The biggest computer programme in the world...ever!': Time for a change in mindset?. *Journal of Information Technology, 22*(3), 212–221.

Cohen, J. (1988). *Statistical power analysis for the behavioral sciences.* Hillsdale, NJ: Lawrence Erlbaum Associates.

Craig, J., & Patterson, V. (2005). Introduction to the practice of telemedicine. *Journal of Telemedicine and Telecare, 11*(1), 3–9.

Creswell, J. W. (2003). *Research design: Qualitative, quantitative, and mixed method approaches.* Thousand Oaks, Calif.: Sage Publications.

Currie, W. L. (2012). Institutional isomorphism and change: The national programme for IT - 10 years on. *Journal of Information Technology, 27*(3), 236–248.

Currie, W. L., & Finnegan, D. J. (2011, April). The policy-practice nexus of electronic health records adoption in the UK NHS: An institutional analysis. *Journal of Enterprise Information Management, 24*(2), 146–170.

Currie, W. L., & Guah, M. W. (2007). Conflicting institutional logics: A national programme for IT in the organisational field of healthcare. *Journal of Information Technology, 22*(3), 235–247.

Daniels, K., Johnson, G., & de Chernatony, L. (2002, January). Task and institutional influences on managers' mental models of competition. *Organization Studies, 23*(1), 31–62.

Datta, L. (1994, March). Paradigm wars: A basis for peaceful coexistence and beyond. *New Directions for Program Evaluation 61*, 53–70.

Davidson, E., & Chismar, W. (2007). The interaction of institutionally triggered and technology-triggered social structure change: An investigation of computerized physician order entry. *Management Information Systems Quarterly, 31*(4), 739–758.

Della Mea, V. (2001, June). What is e-Health (2): The death of telemedicine? *Journal of Medical Internet Research, 3*(2), e22.

DeVellis, R. F. (2003). *Scale development: Theory and applications.* Thousand Oaks, California: Sage Publications.

Diamantopoulos, A. (2011, June). Incorporating formative measures into covariance-based structural equation models. *MIS Quarterly, 35*(2), 335–358.

Diamantopoulos, A., & Winklhofer, H. (2001). Index construction with formative indicators: An alternative to scale development. *Journal of Marketing Research, 38*(2), 269–277.

Die Zeit. (2002). "Lipobay-Skandal: Desaster ohne Nebenwirkungen (von Harro Albrecht)," in Die Zeit.

Dijkstra, T. K. (2010). Latent variables and indices: Herman Wold's basic design and partial least squares. *Handbook of partial least squares* (pp. 23–46).

DiMaggio, P. J., & Powell, W. W. (1983). The iron cage revisited: Institutional isomorphism and collective rationality in organizational fields. *American Sociological Review, 48*(2), 147–160.

Dowling, G. R., & Staelin, R. (1994). A model of perceived risk and intended risk-handling activity. *Journal of Consumer Research, 21*(1), 119–134.

Dwivedi, Y. K., Wade, M. R., & Schneberger, S. L. (2011). *Information systems theory: Explaining and predicting our digital society* (1st ed.). Berlin: Springer.

Earp, J. B., & Payton, F. C. (2006). Information privacy in the service sector: An exploratory study of health care and banking professionals. *Journal of Organizational Computing and Electronic Commerce, 16*(2), 105–122.

Eckhardt, A., Laumer, S., & Weitzel, T. (2009). Who influences whom? analyzing workplace referents' social influence on IT adoption and non-adoption. *Journal of Information Technology, 24*(1), 11–24.

Edwards, J. R., & Bagozzi, R. P. (2000). On the nature and direction of relationships between constructs and measures. *Psychological methods, 5*(2), 155.

Eisenhardt, K. M. (1989). Building theories from case study research. *Academy of Management Review, 14*(4), 532–550.

European Commission. (2012a, December). *Memo: eHealth Action Plan 2012–2020: Frequently Asked Questions.*

European Commission. (2012b, December). Press *release: Putting patients in the driving seat: A digital future for healthcare.*

Eysenbach, G. (2001, June). What is e-health? *Journal of Medical Internet Research, 3*(2), e20.

Featherman, M. S., & Pavlou, P. A. (2003, October). Predicting e-services adoption: A perceived risk facets perspective. *International Journal of Human-Computer Studies, 59*(4), 451–474.

Ferneley, E. H., & Sobreperez, P. (2006). Resist, comply or workaround? An examination of different facets of user engagement with information systems. *European Journal of Information Systems, 15*(4), 345–356.

Fishbein, M., & Ajzen, I. (1975). *Belief, attitude, intention and behavior: An introduction to theory and research.* Reading, Mass: Addison-Wesley Pub.

Flanigan, T. S., McFarlane, E., & Cook, S. (2008). Conducting survey research among physicians and other medical professionals: A review of current literature. *Proceedings of the Survey Research Methods Section, American Statistical Association*, pp. 4136–47.

Fornell, C., & Bookstein, F. L. (1982, November). Two structural equation models: LISREL and PLS applied to consumer exit-voice theory. *Journal of Marketing Research, 19*(4), 440.

Fornell, C., & Larcker, D. F. (1981, February). Evaluating structural equation models with unobservable variables and measurement error. *Journal of Marketing Research, 18*(1), 39–50.

Gefen, D., Rigdon, E. E., & Straub, D. W. (2011). Editor's comment: An update and extension to SEM guidelines for administrative and social science research. *MIS Quarterly, 35*(2), iii–xiv.

Gefen, D., & Straub, D. (2005, July). A practical guide to factorial validity using PLS-graph: Tutorial and annotated example. *Communications of the Association for Information Systems, 16*(1), 182–217

Gefen, D., Straub, D. W., & Boudreau, M.-C. (2000). Structural equation modeling and regression: Guidelines for research and practice. *Communications of the Association for Information Systems, 4*, 7.

Geisser, S. (1975, June). The predictive sample reuse method with applications. *Journal of the American Statistical Association, 70*(350), 320–328.

Gerbing, D. W., & Anderson, J. C. (1988). An updated paradigm for scale development incorporating unidimensionality and its assessment. *Journal of Marketing Research, 25*, 186–192.

Gesellschaft für Telematikanwendungen der Gesundheitskarte mbh. gematik Unternehmensorganisation, Historie. Retrieved May 5, 2014 from http://www.gematik.de/cms/de/gematik/unternehmensorganisation/historie_1/historie_1.jsp.

Gesellschaft für Telematikanwendungen der Gesundheitskarte mbh, and Booz Allen Hamilton 2006. Kosten-Nutzen-Analyse der Einrichtung einer TelematikInfrastruktur im deutschen Gesundheitswesen.

GKV-Spitzenverband. Alle gesetzlichen Krankenkassen - GKV-Spitzenverband. Retrieved May 5, 2014 from http://www.gkv-spitzenveband.de/krankenversicherung/krankenversicherung_grundprinzipien/alle_gesetzlichen_krankenkassen/alle_gesetzlichen_krankenkassen.jsp.

Goh, J. M., Gao, G. (Gordon), & Agarwal, R. (2011, June). Evolving work routines: Adaptive routinization of information technology in healthcare. *Information Systems Research, 22*(3), 565–585.

Goodhue, D. L., Lewis, W., & Thompson, R. (2012, September). Comparing PLS to regression and LISREL: A response to Marcoulides, Chin, and Saunders. *MIS Quarterly, 36*(3), 703–716.

Götz, O., Liehr-Gobbers, K., & Krafft, M. (2010). Evaluation of structural equation models using the partial least squares (PLS) approach. *Handbook of partial least squares* (pp. 691–711). Berlin Heidelberg: Springer.

Greenhalgh, T., Stramer, K., Bratan, T., Byrne, E., Mohammad, Y., & Russell, J. (2008, October 23). Introduction of shared electronic records: Multi-site case study using diffusion of innovation theory. *BMJ, 337*, a1786.

Greenhalgh, T., Stramer, K., Bratan, T., Byrne, E., Russell, J., Hinder, S., et al. (2010). *The devil's in the detail. Final report of the independent evaluation of the Summary Care Record and Healthspace programmes.* London: University College London.

Grimsley, M., & Meehan, A. (2007, April). e-Government information systems: Evaluation-led design for public value and client trust. *European Journal of Information Systems, 16*(2), 134–148.

Hair, J. F., Celsi, M. W., Money, A. H., Samouel, P., & Page, M. J. (2011). *Essentials of business research methods.* New York: M. E. Sharpe Incorporated.

Hair, J. F, Jr, Hult, G. T. M., & Ringle, C. M. (2013). *A primer on partial least squares structural equation modeling.* Los Angeles: Sage Pubn Inc.

Hair, J. F., Ringle, C. M., & Sarstedt, M. (2011b, April). PLS-SEM: Indeed a silver bullet. *The Journal of Marketing Theory and Practice, 19*(2), 139–152.

Hair, J. F., Sarstedt, M., Ringle, C. M., & Mena, J. A. (2012, May). An assessment of the use of partial least squares structural equation modeling in marketing research. *Journal of the Academy of Marketing Science, 40*(3), 414–433.

Hall, D. T., & Mansfield, R. (1975). Relationships of age and seniority with career variables of engineers and scientists. *Journal of Applied Psychology, 60*(2), 201.

Hanseth, O., & Lyytinen, K. (2010, March). Design theory for dynamic complexity in information infrastructures: The case of building internet. *Journal of Information Technology, 25*(1), 1–19.

Hanseth, O., & Monteiro, E. (1998). Changing irreversible networks: Institutionalisation and infrastructure.

HealthIT.gov. Health IT Adoption Programs. Retrieved May 5, 2014 from http://www.healthit. gov/policy-researchers-implementers/health-it-adoption-programs.

Heart, T., Parmet, Y., Pliskin, N., Zuker, A., & Pliskin, J. S. (2011, March). Investigating physicians' compliance with drug prescription notifications. *Journal of the Association for Information Systems, 12*(3), 235–254.

Herrmann, A., Huber, F., & Kressmann, F. (2006). Varianz- und kovarianzbasierte Strukturgleichungsmodelle : ein Leitfaden zu deren Spezifikation. Schätzung und Beurteilung, *58*, 34–66.

Hinkin, T. R. (1998). A brief tutorial on the development of measures for use in survey questionnaires. *Organizational Research Methods, 1*(1), 104–121.

Hirschheim, R., & Newman, M. (1988). Information systems and user resistance: theory and practice. *Computer Journal, 31*(5), 398–408.

Ho, V. T., Ang, S., & Straub, D. (2003). When subordinates become IT contractors: Persistent managerial expectations in IT outsourcing. *Information Systems Research, 14*(1), 66–86.

Homburg, C. (1992). Die Kausalanalyse: Eine Einführung. *Wirtschaftswissenschaftliches Studium, 21*(10), 499–508.

Homburg, C., & Baumgartner, H. (1995). Beurteilung von Kausalmodellen. Bestandsaufnahme und Anwendungsempfehlungen. *Marketing ZfP, 17*(3), 162–176.

Homburg, C., & Giering, A. (1996). Konzeptualisierung und Operationalisierung komplexer Konstrukte: Ein Leitfaden für die Marketingforschung. *Marketing - Zeitschrift für Forschung und Praxis, 18*(1), 5–24.

Hulland, J. (1999). Use of partial least squares (PLS) in strategic management research: A review of four recent studies. *Strategic Management Journal, 20*(2), 195–204.

Jarvis, C. B., MacKenzie, S. B., & Podsakoff, P. M. (2003). A critical review of construct indicators and measurement model misspecification in marketing and consumer research. *Journal of Consumer Research, 30*(2), 199–218.

Jensen, T. B., Kjærgaard, A., & Svejvig, P. (2009). Using institutional theory with sensemaking theory: A case study of information system implementation in healthcare. *Journal of Information Technology, 24*(4), 343–353.

Jick, T. D. (1979, December). Mixing qualitative and quantitative methods: Triangulation in action. *Administrative Science Quarterly, 24*(4), 602.

Jöreskog, K., & Wold, H. (1982). The ML and PLS techniques for modeling with latent variables: Historical and comparative aspects. In: K. Jöreskog & H. Wold (Eds.), *Systems under indirect observation, part 1* (pp. 263–270).

Joshi, K. (1991). A model of users' perspective on change: The case of information systems technology implementation. *MIS Quarterly, 15*(2), 229–242.

Kahneman, D., & Tversky, A. (1979). Prospect theory: An analysis of decision under risk. *Econometrica: Journal of the Econometric Society, 47*, 263–291.

Kellerman, S. E., & Herold, J. (2001, January). Physician response to surveys: A review of the literature. *American Journal of Preventive Medicine, 20*(1), 61–67.

Kim, H.-W., & Kankanhalli, A. (2009). Investigating user resistance to information systems implementation: A status quo bias perspective. *MIS Quarterly, 33*(3), 567–582.

Klaus, T., & Blanton, J. E. (2010). User resistance determinants and the psychological contract in enterprise system implementations. *European Journal of Information Systems, 19*(6), 625–636.

Klocker, P. (2014, January 06th–09th). Understanding stakeholder behavior in Nationwide Electronic Health infrastructure implementation. In: *Proceedings of the 47th Hawaii International Conference on System Sciences (HICSS), IT Adoption, Diffusion and Evaluation in Healthcare Track*, Koloa, Hawaii, USA, pp. 2857–2866

Kock, N. (2011). Using WarpPLS in e-Collaboration studies: Mediating effects, control and second order variables, and algorithm choices. *International Journal of e-Collaboration, 7*(3), 1–13.

Kohli, R., & Kettinger, W. J. (2004). Informating the clan: Controlling physicians' costs and outcomes. *MIS Quarterly, 28*(3), 363–394.

Kohn, L. T., Corrigan, J., & Donaldson, M. S. (2000). *To error is human: Building a safer health system*. Washington, D.C.: National Academy Press.

Kottke, T. E., Solberg, L. I., Conn, S., Maxwell, P., Thomasberg, M., & Brekke, M. L., et al. (1990, July). A comparison of two methods to recruit physicians to deliver smoking cessation interventions. *Archives of Internal Medicine, 150*(7), 1477–1481.

Kozlowski, S. W. J., & Klein, K. J. (2000). A multilevel approach to theory and research in organizations: Contextual, temporal, and emergent processes. In K. J. Klein & S. W. J. Kozlowski (Eds.), *Multilevel theory, research, and methods in organizations: Foundations, extensions, and new directions* (pp. 3–90). San Francisco, CA, US: Jossey-Bass.

Lapointe, L., & Beaudry, A. (2014, January 06th-09th). Identifying IT user mindsets: Acceptance, resistance and ambivalence. In: *Proceedings of the 47th Hawaii International Conference on System Science*, Koloa, Hawaii, USA.

Lapointe, L., & Rivard, S. (2005). A multilevel model of resistance to information technology implementation. *MIS Quarterly, 29*(3), 461–491.

Lapointe, L., & Rivard, S. (2012). Information technology implementers' responses to user resistance: Nature and effects. *MIS Quarterly, 36*(3), 897–A5.

Lewis, W., Agarwal, R., & Sambamurthy, V. (2003). Sources of influence on beliefs about information technology use: An empirical study of knowledge workers. *MIS Quarterly, 27*(4), 657–678.

Liang, H., Saraf, N., Hu, Q., & Xue, Y. (2007). Assimilation of enterprise systems: The effect of institutional pressures and the mediating role of top management. *MIS Quarterly, 31*(1), 59–87.

Lohmöller, J.-B. (1989). *Latent variable path modeling with partial least squares*. Heidelberg: Springer-Verlag.

MacKenzie, S. B., Podsakoff, P. M., & Podsakoff, N. P. (2011, June). Construct measurement and validation procedures in MIS and behavioral research: integrating new and existing techniques. *MIS Quarterly, 35*(2), 293–334.

Marakas, G., & Hornik, S. (1996). Passive resistance misuse: Overt support and covert recalcitrance in IS implementation. *European Journal of Information Systems, 5*(3), 208–219.

Markus, M. L. (1983). Power, politics, and MIS implementation. *Communications of the ACM, 26*(6), 430–444.

Martinko, M. J., Henry, J. W., & Zmud, R. W. (1996). An attributional explanation of individual resistance to the introduction of information technologies in the workplace. *Behaviour Information Technology, 15*(5), 313–330.

Mateos-Aparicio, G. (2011). Partial least squares (PLS) methods: Origins, evolution, and application to social sciences. *Communications in Statistics - Theory and Methods, 40*(13), 2305–2317.

Meissonier, R., & Houzé, E. (2010). Toward an 'IT conflict-resistance theory': Action research during IT pre-implementation. *European Journal of Information Systems, 19*(5), 540–561.

Mekonnen, S. M., & Sahay, S. (2008). An institutional analysis on the dynamics of the interaction between standardizing and scaling processes: A case study from Ethiopia. *European Journal of Information Systems, 17*(3), 279–289.

Melas, C. D., Zampetakis, L. A., Dimopoulou, A., & Moustakis, V. S. (2013, August). An empirical investigation of technology readiness among medical staff based in Greek hospitals. *European Journal of Information Systems* (advance online publication).

Mignerat, M., & Rivard, S. (2012, April). The institutionalization of information system project management practices. *Information and Organization, 22*(2), 125–153.

Mingers, J. (2001). Combining IS research methods: Towards a pluralist methodology. *Information systems research, 12*(3), 240–259.

Miscione, G. (2007). Telemedicine in the Upper Amazon: Interplay with local health care practices. *MIS Quarterly, 31*(2), 403–425.

Moore, G. C., & Benbasat, I. (1991). Development of an instrument to measure the perceptions of adopting an information technology innovation. *Information Systems Research, 2*(3), 192–222.

Morris, M. G., & Venkatesh, V. (2000, June). Age differences in technology adoption decisions: Implications for a changing work force. *Personnel Psychology, 53*(2), 375–403.

Noir, C., & Walsham, G. (2007). The great legitimizer: ICT as myth and ceremony in the Indian healthcare sector. *Information Technology & People, 20*(4), 313–333.

Nunnally, J. C., & Bernstein, I. H. (1994). *Psychometric theory* (3rd ed.). New York: McGraw-Hill.

Okoli, C., & Schabram, K. (2010). A guide to conducting a systematic literature review of information systems research. *Sprouts: Working Papers on Information Systems* (10:26).

Oliver, C. (1991, January). Strategic responses to institutional processes. *The Academy of Management Review, 16*(1), 145–179.

Overby, E. (2008). Process virtualization theory and the impact of information technology. *Organization Science, 19*(2), 277–291.

Patton, M. Q. (2002). *Qualitative research and evaluation methods.* Thousand Oaks, USA: SAGE.

Paulus, W., & Romanowski, S. (2009). *Telemedizin und AAL in Deutschland: Geschichte.* Forschung Aktuell: Stand und Perspektiven.

Pavlou, P. A. (2011). State of the information privacy literature: Where are we now and where should we go? *MIS Quarterly, 35*(4), 977.

Petter, S., Straub, D., Rai, A. (2007, December). Specifying formative constructs in information systems research. *MIS Quarterly, 31*(4), 623–656.

Podsakoff, P. M., MacKenzie, S. B., Lee, J.-Y., & Podsakoff, N. P. (2003). Common method biases in behavioral research: A critical review of the literature and recommended remedies. *Journal of Applied Psychology, 88*(5), 879–903.

Reichardt, C. S., & Rallis, S. F. (1994, March). Qualitative and quantitative inquiries are not incompatible: A call for a new partnership. *New Directions for Program Evaluation, 61*, 85–91.

Ridenour, C. S., Newman, I. (2008). *Mixed methods research: Exploring the interactive continuum.* Carbondale: SIU Press.

Rigdon, E. E. (1994). Demonstrating the effects of unmodeled random measurement error. *Structural Equation Modeling: A Multidisciplinary Journal, 1*(4), 375–380.

Rindfleisch, T. C. (1997). Privacy, information technology, and health care. *Communications of the ACM, 40*(8), 92–100.

Ringle, C. M., Sarstedt, M., & Straub, D. W. (2012, March). Editor's comments: A critical look at the use of PLS-SEM in MIS quarterly. *MIS Quarterly, 36*(1), iii–xiv.

Ringle, C., Wende, S., & Will, A. (2005). *SmartPLS.* Hamburg, Germany: SmartPLS.

Rivard, S., Lapointe, L., & Kappos, A. (2011, February). An organizational culture-based theory of clinical information systems implementation in hospitals. *Journal of the Association for Information Systems, 12*(2), 1–40.

Rogers, E. M. (1962). *Diffusion of innovations* (1st ed.). New York: Free Press.

Romanow, D., Sunyoung C., & Straub, D. (2012). Riding the wave: Past trends and future directions for health IT research. *MIS Quarterly, 36*(3), iii–A18.

Rossi, P. H. (1994, March). The war between the quals and the quants: Is a lasting peace possible? *New Directions for Program Evaluation, 61,* 23–36.

Rossiter, J. R. (2002). The C-OAR-SE procedure for scale development in marketing. *International journal of research in marketing, 19*(4), 305–335.

Sahay, S., Aanestad, M., & Monteiro, E. (2009). Configurable politics and asymmetric integration: Health e-Infrastructures in India. *Journal of the Association for Information Systems, 10*(5), 399–414.

Samuelson, W., & Zeckhauser, R. (1988). Status quo bias in decision making. *Journal of Risk and Uncertainty, 1,* 7–59.

Scott, W. R. (2001). *Institutions and organizations.* Los Angeles, Calif.: Sage Publications.

Silva, L., & Backhouse, J. (2003, November). The circuits-of-power framework for studying power in institutionalization of information systems. *Journal of the Association for Information Systems, 4,* 1.

Smith, H. J., Dinev, T., & Xu, H. (2011, December). Information privacy research: An interdisciplinary review. *MIS Quarterly, 35*(4), 989–1016.

Spiegel Online. (2014, March). Umfrage: Hunderttausende besitzen noch keine elektronische Gesundheitskarte, in Spiegel Online.

Statistisches Bundesamt. (2013a, January). Gesundheit - Ausgaben - Fachserie 12 Reihe 7.3.1 - 2011.

Statistisches Bundesamt. (2013b, October). Gesundheit - Grunddaten der Krankenhaeuser - Fachserie 12 Reihe 6.1.1 - 2012.

Statistisches Bundesamt. (2014, April). Gesundheitsausgaben 2012 übersteigen 300 Milliarden Euro - Pressemitteilung vom 7. April 2014 – 126/14.

Stone, M. (1974). Cross-validatory choice and assessment of statistical predictions. *Journal of the Royal Statistical Society Series B (Methodological), 36*(2), 111–147.

Tashakkori, A., & Teddlie, C. (2003). Issues and dilemmas in teaching research methods courses in social and behavioural sciences: US perspective. *International Journal of Social Research Methodology, 6*(1), 61–77.

Taylor, S., & Todd, P. A. (1995, June). Understanding information technology usage: A test of competing models. *Information Systems Research, 6*(2), 144–176.

Teo, H. H., Wei, K. K., & Benbasat, I. (2003). Predicting intention to adopt interorganizational linkages: An institutional perspective. *MIS Quarterly, 27*(1), 19–49.

Van Offenbeek, M., Boonstra, A., & Seo, D. (2013, July). Towards integrating acceptance and resistance research: Evidence from a telecare case study. *European Journal of Information Systems, 22*(4), 434–454.

VanGeest, J. B., Johnson, T. P., & Welch, V. L. (2007, December). Methodologies for improving response rates in surveys of physicians a systematic review. *Evaluation & the Health Professions, 30*(4), 303 321.

Venkatesh, V. (2000). Determinants of perceived ease of use: Integrating control, intrinsic motivation, and emotion into the technology acceptance model. *Information Systems Research, 11*(4), 342–365.

Venkatesh, V., Brown, S. A., & Bala, H. (2013). Bridging the qualitative-quantitative divide: Guidelines for conducting mixed methods research in information systems. *MIS Quarterly, 37*(1), 21–54.

Venkatesh, V., & Davis, F. D. (2000). A theoretical extension of the technology acceptance model: Four longitudinal field studies. *Management Science, 46*(2), 186–204.

Venkatesh, V., Morris, M. G., Davis, G. B., & Davis, F. D. (2003). User acceptance of information technology: Toward a unified view. *MIS Quarterly, 27,* 425–478.

Venkatesh, V., Zhang, X., & Sykes, T. A. (2011). 'Doctors do too little technology': A longitudinal field study of an electronic healthcare system implementation. *Information Systems Research, 22*(3), 523–546.

Walsham, G. (2006, June). Doing interpretive research. *European Journal of Information Systems,* *15*(3), 320–330.

Walter, Z., & Lopez, M. S. (2008). Physician acceptance of information technologies: Role of perceived threat to professional autonomy. *Decision Support Systems, 46*(1), 206–215.

Webster, J., & Watson, R. T. (2002). Analyzing the past to prepare for the future: Writing a literature review. *MIS Quarterly, 26*(2), xiii–xxiii.

Williams, M. D., Dwivedi, Y. K., Lal, B., & Schwarz, A. (2009). Contemporary trends and issues in IT adoption and diffusion research. *Journal of Information Technology, 24*(1), 1–10.

Wold, H. (1975). *Path models with latent variables: The NIPLAS approach.* New York: Academic Press.

Wunderlich, P. (2013*). Green information systems in the residential sector: An examination of the determinants of smart meter adoption.* New York: Springer.

Xu, H., Dinev, T., Smith, J., & Hart, P. (2011, December). Information privacy concerns: Linking individual perceptions with institutional privacy assurances. *Journal of the Association for Information Systems, 12*(12), 798.